GEOFF HURST'S GREATS

England's 1966 Hero Selects his Finest Ever Footballers

**1966 WORLD CUP
50th ANNIVERSARY
EDITION**

IN ASSOCIATION WITH
TIMPSON

GEOFF HURST'S GREATS

England's 1966 Hero Selects his Finest Ever Footballers

1966 WORLD CUP 50th ANNIVERSARY EDITION

SIR GEOFF HURST

This edition published in the UK in 2016 by
Icon Books Ltd, Omnibus Business Centre,
39–41 North Road, London N7 9DP
email: info@iconbooks.com
www.iconbooks.com

First published in the UK in 2014 by Icon Books Ltd

Sold in the UK, Europe and Asia
by Faber & Faber Ltd, Bloomsbury House,
74–77 Great Russell Street,
London WC1B 3DA or their agents

Distributed in the UK, Europe and Asia
by Grantham Book Services,
Trent Road, Grantham NG31 7XQ

Distributed in the USA by
Publishers Group West,
1700 Fourth Street, Berkeley, CA 94710

Distributed in Australia and New Zealand
by Allen & Unwin Pty Ltd,
PO Box 8500, 83 Alexander Street,
Crows Nest, NSW 2065

Distributed in South Africa by
Jonathan Ball, Office B4, The District,
41 Sir Lowry Road, Woodstock 7925

Distributed in Canada by Publishers Group Canada,
76 Stafford Street, Unit 300
Toronto, Ontario M6J 2S1

ISBN: 978-178578-050-9

Typeset and designed by Simmons Pugh

Printed and bound in the UK by Clays Ltd, St Ives plc

To my wife, Judith, daughters and grandchildren for all they give to me and to whom I hope this possibly but only very occasionally grumpy old man has shown and will continue to show more than just a token of his great appreciation, thanks and love.

ABOUT THE AUTHOR

Sir Geoff Hurst MBE is the only man to score a hat-trick in a World Cup final – for England in their historic 4-2 victory over West Germany at Wembley in 1966.

Having shown an early flair for cricket – playing a first-class match for Essex against Lancashire in 1962 – Hurst opted for a career in football, and with West Ham United he scored 248 goals in 499 first team appearances. There he won the FA Cup in 1964 and the European Cup Winners' Cup in 1965. He was selected by Alf Ramsey to lead England's attack between 1966 and 1972, the longest run of any forward under Ramsey, scoring 24 goals in that time. After three seasons with Stoke he finished his Football League career with West Bromwich Albion in 1976.

Hurst enjoyed stints in the USA (Seattle Sounders) and Ireland (Cork Celtic) before returning to England to manage non-league Telford United and then Chelsea, and in recent years he has travelled with the England team. He lives in Cheltenham.

CONTENTS

INTRODUCTION

W ell, this was easy, wasn't it? I have lost count of how many drafts I have produced and how many family members and friends have not so politely suggested that my choices were possibly incorrect! So, in spite of all the criticism and abuse, I have made my selection and it may be only me but I think it is pretty good.

So how did I choose my Top 50 Players? Many of course I have played with and known for a long time. And the others? Most have risen to fame since I stopped playing in 1978 and I have watched and enjoyed them on numerous occasions.

There is of course a very personal bias. The majority are forwards. Eleven of them are English. Five are teammates from the 1966 World Cup final squad. But that leaves 35 other players in all other positions and somehow, in some undefinable way, I have ranked them all.

What I think all these players have in common is that something special that elevates them above the mere mortal or indeed very good. (And that, in case you may be wondering, includes me. Yes, I may be the only person ever to have scored a hat-trick in a World Cup final and yes, I may have been an integral part of probably this country's greatest ever sporting moment, but would I be in my Top 50? I do not think so. And this is not false modesty.)

All these players could do something special – something that could win or save a match – and they did so on a regular basis. And these are all players for whom I would happily pay the price of a match ticket – preferably the old-fashioned price – to go and watch. And it is a funny thing about 'greatness' – which is what I think all these 50 have to varying degrees – and that is, it is something which, when displayed in whatever walk of life, we can somehow all recognise. So I would like to think that even non-football lovers might appreciate some of the talents of my chosen!

So a big thank you to all those who have helped and abused me in creating my list and I will not take it too personally if you, the reader, disagree with all or any of it. Even now, as I look down the list of possible substitutes, I start to re-question my choice. But here it is, and I hope you enjoy reading about and recalling some of the greatest players and moments in the history of football and my personal take on them all.

I wish you very happy reading and hope I do not cause too many conflicts in the process.

All the best

GH

GEOFF HURST'S GREATS

50. PAOLO MALDINI

Who better to kick off the 50 with than Paolo Maldini? An exemplary professional and a fantastic footballer, he'd be in the shortlist for anybody's greatest ever XI. This is probably the time to point out that my selection has an unashamed attacking slant, and that if you were to select an XI based on this list then you'd probably end up playing a 2-3-5 formation. The upshot of this is that any defender to make it into the list is or was a class act.

Following in the footsteps of his father, AC Milan legend Cesare Maldini, when a young Paolo joined the ranks expectations were unrealistically high. Or so you would have been forgiven for thinking. Maldini senior had enjoyed more than a decade at the club, winning four Serie A titles and one European Cup during his stay. The pressure wasn't helped by the fact that Paolo showed an early flair for defending, with his father fondly remembered as a confident ball-playing centre back for Milan.

After standing out from his teammates in the youth team, in early 1985 at the age of just sixteen he was thrust into the first team by manager Nils Liedholm. Though he never once showed signs of nerves during his long career, Maldini later admitted he'd hoped that Liedholm wouldn't bring him on, so intimidated was he by the prospect of running out in front of the San Siro crowd. Injuries had left Milan short of bodies in defence and Paolo was drafted in for half a game as the crisis escalated. Playing at right

back, he made enough of an impression in his brief debut that he was handed a starting place at the beginning of the following season.

From that point on, Maldini didn't look back. Even at just seventeen, the composure he showed both with the ball at his feet and when defending was exceptional. I don't mean exceptional for a seventeen-year-old either. His reading of the game far exceeded that of many seasoned professionals, and this gave him far more time at his disposal than looked possible. I remember seeing him casually weaving his way out of defence as though he were meandering over the halfway line, something any manager would berate a young defender for doing, but Paolo never looked pressured.

His third full season brought with it his first Serie A title in a fiercely competitive league and his fourth and fifth each brought a European Cup. His achievements by the age of 21 would have satisfied most people as an entire career's worth but Paolo Maldini is not most people.

Exceedingly accomplished in defence, he was just as much of an asset going forward. As well as chipping in with a few goals in most seasons, his overlapping play on the left was particularly key to Milan's success. Often favouring a narrow midfield, his pace and crossing ability in his early years was invaluable. Having said that, in terms of his career span, his 'early years' could stretch into his thirties, which just goes to illustrate the longevity of his tenure in one of football's most steely defences.

In recent years Sir Alex Ferguson admitted that he had made a number of sustained approaches to recruit him to Manchester United but to no avail. In true Italian fashion, Maldini's commitment to his club extended beyond that of an employee, regarding his colleagues almost as family. This was partly due to his father's career before him at the club and Paolo remained staunchly loyal for 24 years, making 647 Serie A appearances, winning seven Serie A titles and five European Cups.

One thing that evaded Paolo in his long career was international success with Italy, just missing out on the victorious 2006 tournament as he was deemed to be surplus to requirements. This might have been somewhat harsh but Italy's victory appeared to justify it. After 126 caps, 74 as captain, it was an agonising turn of events. Despite numerous other disappointments, his spell with the national side was anything but dull.

Italy were beaten finalists in 1994 but the 1998 World Cup was noteworthy for different reasons. Extending the scope of their footballing dynasty, Maldini senior and junior linked up for the Azzurri, with Cesare taking the reins as manager. Unlike most father/son management arrangements, there was absolutely no danger of claims of favourable treatment with Paolo firmly established as an essential pick. A penalty shootout defeat against hosts and eventual winners France in the quarter-finals sent them packing. A disappointing if respectable end.

His was a one-club career that is almost out-dated in the modern era. An evergreen player of the utmost quality, Paolo Maldini left a legacy to trump all legacies. The left back of choice in world football for two decades, he continued Milan's proud European and domestic traditions, leaving the famous club with a reputation even more distinguished than when he signed.

49. FABIO CANNAVARO

Okay, so maybe I've been more generous to defenders than I'd let on, but in Fabio Cannavaro we have another stellar Italian talent. In 2006 when Italy lifted the World Cup in Germany, Cannavaro was utterly peerless. I will always prefer the sight of a goal scored over a successful challenge, but when he was at his peak it was hard not to enjoy the sight of him completely disarming forwards who were visibly panicking at the prospect of having to find a way past – if only because I wasn't said forward.

The entire 2005/06 season was an astonishing story in itself, and Cannavaro took centre stage in a year that ended in absolute chaos. Having played a starring role as Juventus walked to the title, he was voted Serie A's Defender of the Year for the second season running and won the Serie A Player of the Year title too. He had been a rock for them all season, something that nobody disputed.

However, with all tied up in the league and as the World Cup neared, whispers about match-fixing began to spread through the Italian media. Five teams found themselves under scrutiny: Fiorentina, AC Milan, Lazio, Reggina and Cannavaro's Juventus. The allegations refused to go away and in early July as the World Cup began it became clear that serious wrongdoing had occurred, the suggestion being that the clubs had used bribes to ensure favourable refereeing. Of course, Cannavaro had nothing to do with this.

As the tournament in Germany gathered pace, so did the media storm back home, spreading across the globe as football's greatest show vied with one of its most shameful

episodes to grab the headlines. All the while, Cannavaro and his Italian teammates played on, with several of them not knowing what state their club sides would be in when they returned. Admittedly, Cannavaro's form was enough to ensure that there would be no end of potential suitors lining up should Juventus face the suggested punishment of relegation, but it was still a hugely unwelcome distraction during one of the most important months of his life.

If he was preoccupied with the scandal, it certainly didn't show on the pitch. In fact the longer Calciopoli raged on, the more determined the Italian team became. Topping their group with only one goal conceded, Cannavaro's influence in the defence was telling. As team captain, he showed the type of resilience that you can't help but admire, even when the fallout escalated in Italy as Gianluca Pessotto, a former teammate and a director at Juventus, attempted to commit suicide.

Somehow, amidst all of this disturbance, Cannavaro continued to perform as Italy forced their way into the final against France, a repeat of the Euro 2000 final six years earlier. In their three knockout games en route to the final they kept three further clean sheets, including a 2-0 victory over Germany that stretched to 120 minutes.

The final was overshadowed by another scandalous act, a momentary loss of cool from Zidane with an astonishing headbutt on Marco Materazzi, but by this time I'm not sure anything could have stolen the Italians' focus. The game was decided on penalties after goals from the headbutter and the headbuttee and saw the game end 1-1. Italy didn't miss a single penalty, completing the most unlikely of triumphs.

As many had believed necessary but didn't think likely, in addition to their relegation to Serie B, Juventus were stripped of their title and that from the previous season. Cannavaro promptly moved to Real Madrid and continued to win plaudits, escaping relatively unscathed from the whole sorry affair.

The World Cup win was no more than Cannavaro deserved as his two years with Juventus were effectively erased from the history books. Even so, it's important to stress that his performances throughout his time in Turin were not the product of match-fixing; the opposition's attackers would still have failed to get past him had the referees remained completely impartial.

While a whole host of figures from the Italian footballing scene were shamed by the events, it was most pleasing to see that Cannavaro was recognised as an unwitting pawn in their game. He finished 2006 with the Ballon d'Or and FIFA's World Player of the Year award to his name, as he exerted the same steadying effect over Real Madrid as he had over the Italian national side. The leadership skills he showed over the course of that turbulent year surpassed all expectations, revealing a strength of character that is only found in the very greatest of players.

48. ANDRÉS INIESTA

Throughout Barcelona's reign of supremacy under Pep Guardiola's management and beyond, three players were hailed above all others as symbols of perfection. Countless articles and hours of television analysis were dedicated to three men with a wide range of qualities but the same core strengths. Having each risen through the ranks at Barcelona's famous La Masia academy, the trio had learned

to play football 'the Barcelona way', beautifully, often simply but always devastatingly effectively.

The star of the generation – both at Barcelona and in football as a whole – was Lionel Messi, but the two supporting men haven't been far off. For more than a decade now, Xavi Hernández and Andrés Iniesta have been a bewitching presence in two of the most successful midfields ever. For Barcelona and for Spain the pair have displayed the near-telepathic understanding that can usually only be nurtured over the course of a lifetime.

Like all good partnerships in football, they each bring something very different to the game. Xavi has become renowned for his passing, both short and long distance. His vision, first and foremost, to read the game and to know where gaps are going to appear, where channels are going to close up and where teammates are going to move cannot be taught. Then to have the ability to act on this understanding, well, that just makes for something quite extraordinary. The result of this, especially when talents such as Messi, David Villa or Samuel Eto'o have been playing ahead of him, is that even the tightest of defences can be left in tatters from the most innocuous of situations.

Rather frighteningly, while Xavi was long considered the best in the world when it came to passing, Iniesta really wasn't that far behind, although excelling particularly over shorter distances. Iniesta's box of attacking tricks is essentially bottomless. He has long delighted in making defenders look quite simple as he jimmies his way through invisible gaps, leaving them dumbfounded as he emerges on the other side.

The most endearing element of the duo, and of Lionel Messi, is their absolute lack of ego. For all their wondrous talent, they exude an air of humility, and this is to the credit of Barcelona's youth system. When you look at exactly what they've achieved in an era when even lower league footballers can become minor celebrities it's astonishing that they've kept such a level head. This has of course been vital to their consistency, never pausing to revel in their success.

At the age of 21, at the end of his first full season in the starting line-up, Andrés Iniesta had a La Liga title to his name. By the end of the following year he had added another along with his first Champions League winner's medal. And so it continued until in 2008 the Midas touch of Barcelona's core spread to the international scene with Spain winning the European Championships, their first major trophy in more than four decades.

His crowning glory came two years later in 2010, as Spain again found themselves challenging for a major honour – this time with the chance to claim their first ever World Cup. It was a bitterly close match against the Netherlands in which tempers frayed, chances were squandered and the game entered into extra time. With fewer than five minutes separating them from a shootout that was starting to look inevitable, Iniesta showed he had other ideas. Finding himself in space inside the area, his agile mind still ticking over while others had slowed through exhaustion, he calmly swept the ball beyond Maarten Stekelenburg to complete his set: Spanish league and cup, Champions League and Super Cup, European Championship and World Cup.

As a player who has never been one to chase individual honours, always working for the team, his individual accolades speak volumes. Placing 2nd (2010), 4th (2011) and 3rd (2012) in the Ballon d'Or voting over three consecutive years, each time with Messi winning and with Xavi finishing ahead of him on one occasion, the three players have benefited from one another's support. It's rare to find such talents in one generation, let alone in one team, and the combination has been absolutely breath-taking at times.

It feels almost unfair to leave Xavi out of this list but with so many greats to include, his exclusion really highlights the difficulty of the task. It will come as no surprise that Lionel Messi features higher up this list, but it's fair to say he has Iniesta and Xavi to thank for that. Equally, Iniesta's placement is in no small part down to this partnership. So at number 48 I have Andrés Iniesta – but with Xavi in support – his World Cup-winning striking proving to be the deciding factor.

47. LEV YASHIN

When recalling the career of Lev Yashin while working on this book, my wife Judith reminded me of the most striking thing about him – he always dressed entirely in black. It may sound daft but so much of a goalkeeper's game is based on looking big and imposing, and he was the very best at doing that. For any striker bearing down on goal to look up and see this dark tower ahead of them, the goal would start to look very small.

Yashin's success was based on more than just looking the part; an often unbeatable force, he patrolled his entire area in a manner reminiscent of the sweeper-keeper style that Manuel Neuer got such recognition for when playing in Brazil 2014. He reimagined a position that most thought had been fully explored and he did so solely at Dynamo Moscow. Spending 22 years with the club from his city of birth, each time the Soviet Union appeared in a World Cup the

world watched eagerly to see the mysterious man in black play.

His only international honour was the inaugural European Championship in 1960, which was contested by four nations: the Soviet Union, Czechoslovakia, Yugoslavia and hosts France. It was a much scaled down version of the competition as we know it today but, coming two years after their World Cup debut and their first Olympic football gold medal, it confirmed the Soviets as a new force in football, albeit as an unknown quantity.

Yashin was their star player and he became recognised as more than just the man between the posts. He was an outspoken personality, always willing to oblige with a good quote or two, and he was outspoken on the pitch too, marshalling the defence with his booming voice. On the face of it, everything he did seemed to be ahead of its time, a precursor for the modern player. That was except for his warm-up routine. He proudly advised all who would listen of his foolproof approach to conditioning, saying, 'The trick is to smoke a cigarette to calm your nerves and then take a big swig of strong liquor to tone your muscles.' Though he certainly wasn't the only one who warmed up in this manner, I'd like to see the scientific research behind the muscle-toning effects he mentions.

His performances drew comment from countless players too. Italy and Inter Milan legend Sandro Mazzola once commented, 'Yashin plays football better than me.' These words came after an Italy vs. USSR fixture in '63, in which Yashin had saved a Mazzola. Though the records are shaky, it is believed he saved over 150 penalties in his career. Whether this is rumour, myth or otherwise, the truth of Mazzola's comments extended beyond the spot kick. The Soviet stopper pioneered techniques of distribution, broadening the role of a goalkeeper. Involving an eleventh player in the outfield game made for a much more comprehensive unit that could turn defence into attack in the blink of an eye.

Yashin's contribution to Dynamo Moscow, Soviet-Russian football and the game as a whole did not go unnoticed. In 1963 he won the Ballon d'Or for his performances. To say this was unprecedented would be an understatement and even to this day he remains the only goalkeeper to win the award. It further highlights his revolution of the position, because before and largely since his playing days the goalkeeper has tended to be a support act in many people's eyes. He showed that they could and should be far more than that.

His testimonial, held in 1971, was final confirmation of his success in transcending the expectations of a stopper. More than 100,000 people turned up to wave him off and the likes of Pelé, Franz Beckenbauer and Eusébio all turned out to play. It drew a bigger crowd than most competitive games and far more than almost any testimonial, but wherever the man in black went, you couldn't help but watch.

46. JOHNNY HAYNES

There's a crop of players whose names are so ingrained in English footballing history that they take on a status greater than that of a player, figures such as Sir Stanley Matthews and Nat Lofthouse who pre-dated the era of professionalism and celebrity, playing simply for the love of the game.

With only a handful of televised matches and no first-hand experiences to steer my opinion of these players, it's hard for me to place them in a list like this. Undoubtedly they would

feature in many people's list of 50 greatest players and I feel they're worthy of the most honourable of mentions, but any placement I could give them would be guesswork.

One player closer to my generation who I'm not prepared to overlook, however, is Fulham's Johnny Haynes. Known as The Maestro, he became the first ever player to earn £100 a week, a sign of his worth in modest times. He was clearly in it for more than just money too as he spent seventeen years at the London club, playing 594 times and scoring 146 times.

His name is synonymous with a time when rewards for ability were deemed acceptable, when star players earned what they were worth to their fans and community (shock horror!). As the captain of England and one of the stars in the English First Division he was a genuine superstar.

Beginning his time at Fulham at the age of fifteen when they were a Second Division outfit, he helped forge a route to success for the club. Haynes was an inspirational player, leading both by example and vocally, never afraid to let his teammates know when they were underperforming. He was an exceptional passer of the ball with great vision, which also manifested itself in his wonderful attacking positioning.

It's no surprise then that he was playing a commanding role for England while he attempted to lift Fulham to the top flight, having done more than enough to convince all who saw him of his abilities. The inside forward soon became known throughout the land and raised the profile of Fulham as a result. In a 56-game career with the national side he scored eighteen times while captaining the side on 22 occasions. Enjoying a number of very good matches in an England shirt, his finest moment came in 1958 with a hat-trick against Russia at Wembley. He was also captain throughout the 1962 World Cup in Chile where England were knocked out by the eventual champions, Brazil.

To put his ability into context, two opinions involving the great Pelé can be called on. Firstly, his and my former teammate George Cohen declared after Haynes' death in 2005, 'He was the best ball-to-foot player I ever saw. If you compared him to Pelé, you won't be far wrong.' A huge statement, but coming from a teammate, one might expect this to be skewed by personal bias and affection, in which case I'd refer you to comments from Pelé himself, who said of Haynes: '[He was the] best passer of the ball I've ever seen.' For a player who played half his career in England's second tier, that's not bad going.

45. GARRINCHA (Manuel Francisco dos Santos)

In his homeland of Brazil there is little doubt that Garrincha was one of the greats, his name regularly held up alongside the likes of Pelé, Maradona and Cruyff. Elsewhere Garrincha is almost mythical, 'The Little Bird' who lived in Pelé's shadow.

Born with a crooked spine, one knock-knee and the other bow-legged, it's a miracle that Garrincha even managed to play the game, let alone to the level he did. It was almost as though his malformed gait was designed for playing football. Seven years Pelé's senior, the two played together between 1957 and '66 for the national side with the unbelievable occurring every time they took to the field.

With Pelé terrorising defences, Garrincha revelled in wing play. It wasn't uncommon to see him beat his man two, three times or more, spurred on by jubilant cheers of the crowd like a bull-fighter toying with his victim. And much like a bull-fight where the torero dazzles and dazes the bull with his red rag, Garrincha's crooked legs often looked like an optical illusion. It was often plain to see that when he gained possession the last thing on his mind was actually forcing a goal-scoring opportunity; he simply delighted in the sparring that came first.

Don't be mistaken though: when Garrincha wanted to win he could split defences with ease. His pace was frightening and his legs gave him an unusually low centre of gravity, making it unfeasibly easy for him to weave through defences and whip crosses in when almost horizontal. He proved just how deadly he could be when he came up against England at the World Cup in Chile in 1962. The matchup came in the quarter-finals en route to Brazil's claiming of the title.

Having scraped through the group on goal average, England were really no match for a Brazil side, even one missing an injured Pelé. It really didn't matter with Garrincha in full flow. The misty conditions on the day only added to the mystique surrounding Garrincha. He was a soloist and for much of the game his teammates just let him get on with it, the English defence running scared. He opened the scoring with a huge leaping header from a corner before Vavá grabbed the second, tucking away the rebound from Garrincha's shot. It was the third goal that really stole the show though.

After nearly an hour of his showmanship, he pulled off his greatest trick – his trademark grand finale. From a good ten yards or so outside the box, he shuffled the ball out from his feet and struck an unstoppable curling effort high into the top right corner. The banana shot, as it was known, had to be seen to be believed. Bear in mind that he was playing with heavy leather balls and not the balloon-like versions used today. Roberto Carlos' efforts in later years were the closest we've seen, but I can only imagine

the boomerang effect Garrincha might have mustered with such relatively weightless objects.

His life off the pitch sadly lacked much of the joy he demonstrated on it, with an alcohol-related liver condition taking his life aged just 49. It was a tragic loss felt throughout Brazil and the outpouring of grief and respect brought the nation to a standstill. Millions turned out to line the streets as his funeral cortège passed through the streets of Rio de Janeiro. The love felt for him by the people was palpable as the procession had to be stopped on numerous occasions due to overcrowding. Nobody wanted to miss their chance to say farewell to the great man.

Perhaps most telling of all was the tribute paid by the Brazilian Football Association. In a small but appropriate gesture, they announced that they would be renaming one of the dressing rooms at the historic Maracanã stadium in his honour. What initially seemed like a small memorial took on much greater significance when they revealed that the home dressing room would be 'Garrincha' while the away dressing room would be named after Pelé. This alone seems to sum up the legacy of the two players. Both loved immensely by their fellow compatriots, Pelé was the king of world football but Garrincha was the champion of Brazil.

44. ZICO (Arthur Antunes Coimbra)

In terms of the beauty and romance of Brazilian football, there aren't many names that so readily embody this as Zico. There have been better players, Pelé being the obvious choice, but even he didn't seem to have quite the same elegance as Zico. The Brazilians are wonderfully and irrepressibly outspoken about their football and it doesn't take long to realise the love the nation has for Zico. He is the ultimate cult hero in a country not lacking in candidates.

On paper, it's hard to see why. The world's most successful footballing nation, an extended stint in the yellow of Brazil has historically been almost a guarantee of silverware but Zico failed to lift a major international trophy. With so many of his compatriots proudly owning World Cup winner's medals it seems strange that a player whose achievements are comparatively few is the one to be celebrated when there are other more highly decorated alternatives on offer.

A much adored individual in his own right, it was his spell in Brazil's most-loved midfield that cemented his reputation. Joined by Falcão and Sócrates, they dazzled defences with their immaculate ball-control and rangy passing, attacking in a measured yet devastating manner. The opening group stage of the 1982 World Cup pitted them against the Soviet Union, Scotland and New Zealand, three colossal mismatches that saw Brazil progress with maximum points and ten goals to their name, three of which were scored by Zico. Their 'reward' for such blistering form was a place in one of the deadliest Groups of Death in history. As a result of Italy and Argentina's failure to top their opening groups, Brazil ended up worse off than the second-placed Soviet Union who instead faced Belgium and Poland.

First up for Brazil were bitter rivals Argentina who entered the tournament as reigning world champions. They still had the experience of Daniel Passarella, Mario Kempes and Ossie Ardiles, and had added a promising youngster to their roster – a curly-haired kid called Diego Maradona. After losing their opening fixture, Argentina entered the game on

the back of two convincing wins and it looked to be a tough match. A Zico goal after eleven minutes ensured that was not the case. Brazil's midfield tore into Argentina's ageing core with artistry and guile, relenting only a few minutes from time to allow a consolation goal. Brazil won 3-1.

Their second tie represented a more troublesome challenge. For all of Brazil's attacking flair, there were still doubts over their defensive rigidity. The measures taken to accommodate Zico, Falcão and Sócrates left them slightly imbalanced and their right full-back was left particularly exposed as a result. Against Scotland and New Zealand, even Argentina, this could be overcome simply by attacking fast and often, scaring them into submission. Italy were the one team against whom this was not an option.

The complete foil to Brazil's all-out attack, Italian sides have always been built on the most solid of defensive foundations. It almost didn't matter who they selected, you just knew you'd never have an easy route to goal against Italy. Nonetheless, Zico and co. persevered with their attacking approach. It should have come as little surprise then when the painstakingly organised Italians struck early through Paolo Rossi, making light work of Brazil's flimsy formation to kick-start a thrilling encounter.

Within ten minutes Brazil's boldness was rewarded. A scintillating interchange between Sócrates and Zico (the highlight of which was an expertly executed Cruyff Turn from Zico) saw them waltz through Italy's defence before dispatching the ball beyond Dino Zoff – no mean feat.

On 25 minutes Brazil's fallibilities were highlighted once again with a lapse in concentration as a lazy pass from the less celebrated fourth member of their midfield, Toninho Cerezo, let Paolo Rossi in for his second. The game ebbed and flowed almost metronomically, each Brazilian attack prompting a less daring counter. Sure enough, Falcão got in on the action midway through the second half with a magnificent goal from outside the area but Italy were soon on top once more, scoring another preventable goal. A partially cleared corner kick returned goalwards with a hopeful punt back into the box. Paolo Rossi found himself unmarked just yards out and made no mistake, claiming his hat-trick and sending Brazil crashing out.

The goal had major implications for the future of Brazilian football. Many at the time attributed their continued failure to defend to too much emphasis on attack, labelling them as idealistic and naive. The Brazilian public were not in agreement, however, fearing that the upshot of a change of tactics would be the adoption of a more Italian approach. The goals that Zico had scored and laid on throughout that tournament were so eye-catchingly beautiful that most Brazilians were eager to see this expressive style retained, even at the expense of success. In truth, the problems with Brazil's style required only a few less intrusive tweaks – greater balance on the wings and a more defensive-minded holding midfielder – and apart from Brazil's workmanlike performance in 1994 this was the compromise that was reached. Success and beauty in equal measure.

Though his time in a Brazil shirt didn't yield trophies, his style of play embodied his nation's approach to the game perfectly. As is often said, England invented the game of football but Brazil made it beautiful. After watching Zico play, you'd find it hard to argue otherwise.

43. RONALDO (Ronaldo Luís Nazário de Lima)

Il Fenomeno. Nowadays his name is rarely uttered without a qualifier such as 'the Brazilian one' or 'the original' but there was a time when this Ronaldo was the most recognisable face in world football. There is a tinge of disappointment felt by many that such a talent allowed his career to fade so ignominiously out of shape and sight. Yet the highlights and accolades that filled his eight or nine years at the top are more than most achieve in an entire career.

On the back of scintillating performances for Cruzeiro at the age of just seventeen, he travelled with the Brazil squad to USA '94 although he played no part. Following the tournament he secured a move to Europe to play for PSV Eindhoven of the Netherlands, as comparisons to the great Pelé abounded. He replaced the legendary Romário who had enjoyed five successful years at the head of PSV's attack.

Two years later in 1996, having maintained his strike rate from his Cruzeiro days averaging nearly a goal a game, he made the move to Spain, signing for Barcelona in a big-money deal. Following a well-worn path, he once again replaced an outgoing Romário and would work under the tutelage of another former PSV personality, manager Bobby Robson. It was here that he announced his arrival to the world, coping admirably with the pressure that accompanies playing for one of football's most demanding sets of supporters.

The 1996/97 season is firmly embedded in Barcelona folklore thanks mainly to Ronaldo's performances. A total of 47 goals in 51 games sealed a debut season more formidable than surely even he could have hoped for, with some of the most spell-binding trickery and sumptuous finishing the Spaniards had ever seen. His efforts were rewarded with three titles and his first FIFA World Player of the Year award. He was already living a semi-nomadic existence, and another transfer followed at the end of the season as Ronaldo departed the Nou Camp in bitter circumstances.

Failure to renegotiate his contract led to the Brazilian forcing a move to Italian giants Inter Milan. In light of the record-breaking £19.5 million paid for him, he would need to replicate his explosive starts at PSV and Barcelona if he was to live up to the fee, especially with the World Cup in France waiting for him at the end of the season. Even against the firmer defences of Serie A, there was little doubt that he would succeed. He finished the season as second top-scorer in the league, helping to push Inter into the Champions League for the first time since it replaced the European Cup in 1992, and he scored six times en route to lifting the UEFA Cup. His form drew plaudits as he was named World Player of the Year once again.

Ronaldo arrived in France in 1998 as the star attraction, with fans the world over eager to get a glimpse of the mercurial striker. He opened his account in Brazil's second game, breaking clear of the Moroccan defence before unleashing a dipping half-volley from outside the box. He went on to score three more times in his next four games but, following convulsions and a consequent trip to hospital on the day of the match, failed to score in the final as Brazil lost 3-0 to hosts France. It was a disappointing end to the tournament but was just the beginning of Ronaldo's glittering association with the World Cup.

Four years later in Japan and South Korea he made up for the disappointment, playing a starring role once more as Brazil were crowned World Champions for a record fifth time. Making light work of some of the best-known defences

in world football, he scored eight times including two against Germany in the final (one shy of my 1966 hat-trick, I might add!) as he closed in on Gerd Müller's record as the all-time World Cup top-scorer.

He arrived in Germany in 2006 having already chalked up twelve World Cup goals, needing two more to draw level with Müller. But by this time injuries had taken their toll on Ronaldo and dramatic weight gain meant he scarcely even resembled the athletic 21-year-old who had stolen the show at France '98. Sentiment undoubtedly played a part in his inclusion but he still showed flashes of ability, scoring twice against Japan in the group stages before breaking Gerd Müller's record with a fifth-minute strike against the Ghanaians in the first knock-out game. Fifteen World Cup goals is indisputable evidence of greatness, no matter how out of shape the scorer.

Had Ronaldo managed to maintain an acceptable level of fitness in his later years he would undoubtedly have ranked higher in this list, and it is a great shame that he didn't because when he was on form he was unstoppable. The sorry end should not overshadow what was a truly illustrious career, in which he combined astonishing pace, close control and instinctive finishing to consistently produce the most beautiful of goals.

42. BRYAN ROBSON

Not since Bobby Charlton had England or Manchester United seen a midfielder of Bryan Robson's quality. Signed in 1981 by Ron Atkinson from West Bromwich Albion in a joint deal that also brought in Robson's teammate Remi

Moses, Robson was said to have cost roughly £1.5 million of a £2 million price tag. This was a record-breaking fee but by the time Robson left Old Trafford nearly thirteen years later he had shown this sum to be an absolute snip.

He was given the number 7 shirt that had been made so famous by George Best, but showed no sign of nerves. At the age of 24 he was already a considerable talent, but his growth as a player once with Manchester United, playing alongside Ray Wilkins, was phenomenal. I had crossed paths with him briefly during my season at West Brom, when he was still just a little boy with curly hair. He'd come a long way since then, though, and it wasn't long before Wilkins had handed over his captain's armband. By the end of his second season at the club Robson lifted the FA Cup. With two goals already to his name in the final, he was gifted a great chance to bag a hat-trick but instead allowed the team's designated penalty taker, Arnold Mühren, to take it.

He was an essential player in the rebuilding of a side that had lost its way slightly. Two more FA Cup winner's medals followed during the 1980s but the foundations he helped lay set the club up for one of its greatest periods of dominance in English football history, a situation that started to bear fruit in his final few seasons at the club. By the time Sir Alex Ferguson took over in 1986 Robson was already well on his way to establishing himself as 'Captain Marvel', for club and country. His sublime technique was matched only by his stamina and unwavering will, and he became known for late bursting runs from deep to snatch goals.

It wasn't only once opposition had tired that Robson's commitment showed either, as he demonstrated so emphatically for England against France in the 1982 World Cup in Spain. With the game just twelve seconds old, Robson's Manchester United teammate Steve Coppell took

a throw-in deep in the French half. His launched throw was flicked on by Terry Butcher on the edge of the six-yard box and Robson ghosted in to acrobatically steer the ball beyond the French goalkeeper. There were still only 27 seconds on the clock when the ball crossed the line as England got off to the best possible start. In true England fashion, the lead was only maintained for 24 minutes requiring a second Robson strike to retain it in the second half.

On so many occasions throughout his career Robson took it upon himself to almost single-handedly drag his side to victory. Even at their peak in the '90s I'm not sure Manchester United had an individual capable of doing this so effectively. Roy Keane showed glimpses of it, but Robson was almost an amalgam of Keane and Paul Scholes, as a tenacious midfielder who could pass, score, tackle and head a ball. There were times when Robson's domination of midfield made it look like his side had fielded an extra man.

It seems somehow incongruous that one of the greatest players in the history of England's most successful club only has two league titles to his credit. For more than a decade he was the beating heart in Manchester United's midfield, maintaining standards during a turbulent period and driving the club on to their vital first Premier League title under Ferguson. It's entirely feasible that without Robson in the midfield, the club would have collapsed once more under the pressure of a 26-year wait for a league trophy. Had that had happened then Sir Alex would have lost his job rather than be given another chance and the next twenty or so years could have panned out very differently.

Bryan bowed out of Old Trafford on the back of a league and cup double, the perfect parting gift for and from such a great servant. There is perhaps no greater measure of his contribution to the club than the results of a poll carried out in 2011 after Manchester United had usurped Liverpool as the team to win the most top-flight titles in England with their nineteenth championship. Voted for by a whole host of legends from the club's illustrious history, Robson came out on top as Manchester United's greatest ever player. To be placed ahead of such icons as George Best, Bobby Charlton and Duncan Edwards by the men who know best what it takes to play for the great side speaks volumes. He is an inspiration to those who came before him and to all those who have followed.

41. MARTIN PETERS

I've long felt that Martin Peters was one of the most underrated players in England's history, having spent many a year playing alongside him for both West Ham and England. Sir Alf Ramsey once described him as 'ten years ahead of his time', a compliment that almost sounded like an insult at the time but which has come to make more sense in the years since.

Interestingly Martin actually started his career later than most, only coming to the game at the age of twelve or thirteen, whereas the majority of footballers and fans are inseparable from their footballs from the age of five or six. This always seems to cast his career in a strange light because he definitely developed in a different way to most players, especially most English players.

At West Ham he was a very good player, enjoying eight seasons with the club and winning the Cup Winners' Cup during his stay, but he was never what you'd call a standout player. He then moved on to Spurs and followed a similar pattern, winning a few trophies and playing plenty of games. It was only when he moved on to Norwich in the mid-'70s that he was really recognised as the star that he was, later being voted as one of their best ever players, despite being 30-plus years of age.

Ron Greenwood, our manager at West Ham and eventually manager of the national side, maintained that Martin would have been 'a sensation on the Continent'. This assessment of playing styles is a very interesting one because to my mind Martin was a fantastic all-rounder. The curse of being such a versatile player is often that you'll be used in countless different positions and deprived of the opportunity to make any one of them your own. After he had played in every position for West Ham, including keeper, a team photo appeared with his head superimposed onto every player's body.

Playing and training in close proximity to Martin, I got to know his strengths better than most and one thing I knew for certain was that the boy could head a ball; in fact he was probably the best header of the ball at the club. Ron Greenwood badgered Sir Alf to include Martin in the England squad but was continually rebuffed. Eventually Ron, growing ever more frustrated, asked 'Why?' Sir Alf's response was puzzling to say the least. 'I'm not sure about the lad,' he told Ron, 'he can't head a ball.' Proof that even the best make mistakes!

When Martin was finally included in the England setup he made sure that his one-time doubter was firmly converted. If you compare his record to that of other high-profile England midfielders you start to get an understanding of just how consistently and impressively he performed. Martin scored twenty goals in 67 caps with no free kicks or penalties in

that number, whereas David Beckham scored seventeen in 115 and Gerrard took 114 games to score 21, both as regular set-piece takers.

Beckham and Gerrard's contribution to the England side wasn't purely based on goals, but neither was Martin's. All the same, twenty goals in 67 caps is a record that most strikers would be pleased with. It's almost identical to Kevin Keegan's record, for example (21 goals in 63). The point I'm trying to make is that, though Martin was known almost as a Steady Eddie, he was verging on prolific as a goal-scoring midfielder for England while also defending admirably.

He scored important goals for England too, not least our second in the 1966 World Cup final. He enjoys reminding me that my hat-trick would never have been had he not scored the all-important second goal – 'If I hadn't scored the second we'd have been beaten 2-1!' He's not wrong, I suppose, but he was definitely equally important in our quarter-final victory over Argentina. In a goal honed on West Ham's training ground at Chadwell Heath, he played in a lovely near-post cross which I put away for the only goal of the game.

For those of a younger generation who weren't fortunate enough to see him play I would liken his style to that of Glen Hoddle and I suppose this may support Sir Alf's view that he was a decade ahead of his time, as well as Ron Greenwood's that he'd have been more greatly appreciated overseas. Often described as a classy or cultured player, Hoddle took the decision later in his career to move to Monaco as he felt the league was more befitting of his style of play. I can't help but feel that, had Martin had a similar opportunity, then he might have been more widely regarded as the great player that he was.

40. DAVE MACKAY

In 2010 when Jimmy Greaves turned 70, a birthday bash was thrown for him at the O2 Arena in London. All his old teammates were invited to watch and participate in an 'an audience with'-style evening, including seven or eight former Spurs players. It's always great to see old teammates at a get-together, as that camaraderie and social element of the game is something old pros sorely miss. Watching them all catching up, it was like nothing had changed. Even when chatting over cups of tea before the event, the old hierarchies were still plain to see. Most notable of all was the respect they all showed for Dave Mackay. It was clear that they still see him very much as 'the man'.

When Dave spoke they all listened, showing him great respect, even the men in their 70s. This sort of respect never dwindles because it's been earned so diligently, in Dave's case by never shying away in big games and by leading them in the toughest of fixtures. Even though Danny Blanchflower was the captain – and a fantastic one at that – Mackay's attitude was infectious, a leader even without the armband. I can assure you that off the field he's a perfect gentleman and definitely not someone to be frightened of but his reputation as a player precedes him.

In my mind there are two very different Dave Mackays and he excelled in both guises. This played a big part in my decision to include him because he proved his worth in contrasting roles. The first was the blood-and-thunder Dave Mackay who was the driving force in an excellent 1960s Spurs side. Most people will think of this version first: tough-tackling Scot and an all-action left half.

But once his legs had started to go and he departed for Second Division Derby County in 1968, a second Dave Mackay emerged. Many had written him off at the time, expecting him to wind down into retirement, but Dave had defied expectations before and needed little encouragement to do so again.

Five years before his move to Derby he broke his leg in a game against Manchester United. Having almost completed his rehabilitation, nine months later in his first game back – a reserves fixture against Shrewsbury – he broke it again. The first time would have defeated a lot of players but to recover a second time seemed impossible. When he finally returned to first team action you can imagine what everyone thought. That man was indestructible.

So when his time at Tottenham came to an end and Derby's Baseball Ground became his new home, Brian Clough knew exactly what he was getting; a man who could overcome all obstacles. The toll of a twice-broken leg and countless more meaty challenges had started to show, so Clough used him as a sweeper. This is when Mackay's footballing nous really came to the fore.

Operating as the launch-pad for Derby, both tactically and as a club, he stood out as a formidable presence in their defence who could instil calm while triggering attacks. Playing more of his football around the box meant his tackling was shackled somewhat, and as a result people began to focus more on his composed creativity. This had been present throughout his days at Tottenham and many at the club considered him to be their most technically gifted player, but oddly this more defensive position shone a light on it.

Though he was nearing the end of his career, his swansong at Derby was quite brilliant. He helped them to secure promotion in his first season and was also joint winner of the

Football Writers' Association Footballer of the Year, sharing the award with Manchester City's Tony Book.

He'll probably always be best known for that fantastic image of him confronting Leeds United's Billy Bremner with a fistful of the Leeds United captain's shirt. It's a photo that captures a bygone era. Two British icons in their own right, both with reputations as unrepentant hard men who could also play a bit; it's a wonderful piece of nostalgia. However, I'm told that it's a picture Mackay does not like because it portrays him as a thug as opposed to a combative player – a marked difference.

It's this principled approach that made him such an admirable character. Slips of temper were uncharacteristic for Mackay and they were certainly not something he prided himself on. His reputation was built on his resilience of character and body, but his success stemmed from a hugely impressive technical grounding. More than just a hard man, Dave Mackay was and still is 'the man'.

39. KENNY DALGLISH

One of the most telling things about a great player is the way in which his teammates speak about him. Good players will be remembered fondly but great players bring with them the rarest of things in an environment fuelled by bravado and confidence, and that is deference. To see and hear Kenny Dalglish's teammates discussing him is akin to watching a competition winner meeting their idol. This is a striking thing to witness at the best of times, but when

those players are stars in their own right you can't help but take note.

The Liverpool side that Kenny Dalglish became so central to included Alan Hansen, Graeme Souness and Ian Rush – three players whose names are revered at Anfield – winning three European Cups and six First Division titles during his stay. Yet when he arrived, signing from Celtic in 1977, he was met with scepticism by the Liverpool faithful. The reason for this doubt had a lot more to do with the man he was replacing than his own reputation.

From 1971 to 1977, Kevin Keegan was the undisputed king of Anfield and the success he enjoyed at Liverpool had led many fans to consider him irreplaceable. Departing England fresh on the back of a league and European Cup double, he signed for German side Hamburg SV for a British record fee of £500,000. Voted runner-up for the Ballon d'Or in his first year overseas before winning it in the next two, Keegan's form was unrelenting. How do you go about replacing that kind of talent?

Dalglish didn't disappoint. He wore the number 7 shirt that had become so synonymous with his predecessor and his performances soon began to catch the eye. After a goalless debut against Manchester United in the Charity Shield, Dalglish proceeded to score in each of his first four games. Though Liverpool began the season in equally impressive form, they tailed off towards Christmas time and their challenge in the league petered out. In contrast, on their travels in Europe they went from strength to strength.

As Dalglish entered the final match of his debut season with the Reds he had scored 30 goals in all competitions, ten more than the club's top scorer the previous season – Kevin Keegan. The match in question was no end-of-season warm down either, rather a European Cup final against Club

Brugge at Wembley. Liverpool were holders having beaten Borussia Mönchengladbach the previous season. It came as little surprise when Kenny Dalglish scored the winning goal, a cool chip past goalkeeper Birger Jensen. They might not have retained the league title, but Liverpool's supporters were left in little doubt that they'd found a more than capable replacement.

Over the years that followed Dalglish became integral to everything that happened at Liverpool. He matched the eye-catching flair of Keegan while threading the rest of the team together. He made them a far more cohesive unit and enabled players like Ian Rush to flourish. Between 1978 and 1986, the seasons in which Liverpool failed to win the First Division were more noteworthy than those in which they were crowned champions, and with two further European Cups won during this period it's little wonder that Kenny is remembered with such fondness.

With sublime passing, shooting and dribbling abilities, he oozed confidence and often put on master classes for the Anfield crowd as the opposition were simply blown away. He scored 172 goals in 515 appearances for Liverpool, a strike rate which reflects the deeper-lying role he assumed after his first season. I've little doubt that had he taken a more selfish approach then he could have ended up with nearly double that goal tally, but this would likely have seen him collect fewer trophies and winner's medals. To succeed as a player and to succeed as a team often requires two different mindsets and Liverpool's dominance would not have been possible without Dalglish, who possessed both in equal measure.

After a glittering playing career and two stints as manager, it feels very natural to see Kenny leading the way at Anfield. With huge figures such as Bob Paisley and Bill Shankly in their illustrious history, Kenny Dalglish has played his way into the reckoning and into the same realm of greatness. The Kop affectionately refer to him as King Kenny, not because he conquered but because he is seen as the head of the empire. It takes a big player to achieve this at any club but at Liverpool it takes something extra special. A masterful player who was a delight to watch, King Kenny was one of the most complete team players in the history of the game.

38. ALAN BALL

The attribute that set Alan Ball apart from all others is arguably the most desired in the modern game. Having played with him from a young age in the England set-up, I witnessed it up close on a number of occasions.

Before our days as teammates in the senior team, we became good friends playing for the youth teams. As was customary at the time, in the early 1960s we travelled with the under-23 team to Turkey for an end-of-season friendly tour. They were always enjoyable trips and helped get you acclimatised to the routines of travelling with England, but they were still just friendly matches. Following one game for which he was left out of the team, Alan made it clear that he didn't see it quite this way.

After the match Nobby Stiles and I were sharing a drink in our room when Bally came storming in. Utterly incensed at having been dropped for the match, he hurled his boot at the wall behind us with all the frustration of a man who had just lost a cup final. You see for Alan, there were no friendlies when the England shirt was involved. Every match was a chance to represent his nation and as a proud Englishman that was invaluable to him. We all took pride in wearing the shirt, but Alan couldn't differentiate between an end-of-season warm down and a World Cup finals match and he was much the better player for it.

When Sir Alf Ramsey gave him the chance he'd been longing for, a call-up to the senior team in 1965, he made clear his intentions. You'd expect a boy not long turned twenty to be somewhat overawed by their first senior call-up – it's what most schoolboys dream of – but the tenacity within Alan was not to be subdued or humbled. He told Sir Alf, 'You're going to have to tear this shirt off my back if you want it back.'

It was this steely determination that made him such a natural pick for the World Cup squad a year later, as the youngest member of the squad at the age of just 21. It's what kept him going for the 120 minutes of the final, roving about the Wembley pitch impervious to fatigue so that at full-time the verdict for Man of the Match was unanimous, with Sir Alf in full agreement. He told his young midfielder: 'You will never play a better game in your life.' To reach your peak at the tender age of 21 might seem bittersweet for some, but when the peak is as vertigo-inducingly high as this, then normality can still be rather impressive.

His winner's mentality coupled with his undoubted ability was invaluable to teammates, fans and managers, but in the world of football everyone has a price. Shortly after the World Cup, Everton deemed Ball worthy of breaking the British transfer record, paying £110,000 to take him to Goodison Park from Blackpool. He enjoyed great success alongside such Everton greats as Howard Kendall, Colin Harvey, Joe Royle and Tommy Wright, winning the league title in 1969/70 in what is often regarded as Everton's greatest ever team.

Following a six-year stay at the Toffees which saw him play 249 times, he again found himself the subject of a record-breaking transfer. This time a move to the capital beckoned, with Arsenal doubling his previous fee in a £220,000 deal. Though his time at Highbury represented a downturn in fortunes for the club, this I think was due to the departures of a number of key names rather than to a loss of form on Alan's part. In fact his performances set him so much apart from his teammates that in 1974 Bertie Mee decided to make him club captain, the position he had held at Everton.

His career with England ended abruptly, though he still wore his nation's captain's armband proudly and was known as the faithfully-beating heart of a team in decline. He was only 30 at the time of his last call-up but a tumultuous decade was just beginning for the national team. Sir Alf had been dismissed after failing to qualify for the 1974 World Cup and qualification for the 1978 World Cup also evaded his successor, Don Revie. As Alan told Sir Alf at the start of his international career, he would never have willingly given up his place, but it was perhaps a blessing that he didn't have to endure that period when the aim was simply to prevent England's decline. Such a classy player, it just feels fitting that he's associated with England's most successful era, rather than one of its least.

He was one of the country's greatest ever servants and took a degree of pride in his performances that is rare and sought-after today. I would hasten to add, however, that his commitment to the cause was only able to shine as a result of tremendous ability. You can care all you like but if you haven't got the ability to make it pay then you've little chance of being Man of the Match in a World Cup final. Personally, I don't agree with the viewpoint that the latest generation of England players don't care. Sometimes commitment is hidden by nerves or just a more reserved disposition, but I can assure you that those of the latest crop whom I've met most definitely do care.

It was such a sad loss when Alan lost his life in 2007, especially given that he was only 61 years of age. Speaking at Martin Peters' induction into the National Hall of Fame shortly before his death, it was clear that his love of the game had not waned, when he said, 'It is one of the proudest moments in your life when someone calls to say you are in the Hall of Fame. Words cannot describe it.' When Alan was himself inducted in 2003 it was a greatly deserved accolade and I'm so pleased that it was announced while he was still alive to enjoy it.

37. PAUL GASCOIGNE

Some players are able to excite and thrill, others can infuriate and annoy, but precious few can make you laugh. Paul Gascoigne played football like the most talented of toddlers, delighting in the game each time he played. In the same way that critics feared curbing Wayne Rooney's temper would curb his talent, there was no way you could send Gazza out and urge him to 'go easy'.

On a few occasions this counted against him, not least in the Italia '90 semi-final against Germany where he over-enthusiastically lunged into a challenge and incurred a suspension-triggering booking. We all remember the tears and most will recall the ill-fated end to that match but whereas many players would have been pilloried for their

loss of composure, with Gazza we could all understand. He was wrapped up in the same emotion we were all feeling at the time, battling for every single ball.

We could also tolerate these self-destructive moments because we all knew that when this unbridled eagerness was harnessed in the right way it could be absolutely spectacular. His goal at Wembley against Scotland in Euro '96 was one of the best goals ever scored in an England shirt. It was a flash of brilliance, though not without precedent, and it displayed so many of the elements that made him great.

He had an ability that seems to have died out in the years since – to run at defenders and get past them. For some reason this has been coached out of players, dismissed as fanciful schoolyard ignorance with the message: 'Why risk dribbling and losing possession when you can pass it?' But that goal against Scotland couldn't be coached, and no combination of passes could bring about the pandemonium that Gazza's solo-effort sparked. Driving at the defence with unshakeable determination made what looked impossible to most observers appear effortless.

The goal – a jinking chase that made it look as though the ball was strung to his foot – was the result of utter fearlessness and would be beyond the abilities of many of history's greatest midfielders. His deftness of touch, looping the ball over Colin Hendry's head with his left boot before lashing home with his right, was simply breathtaking to watch.

The image of his return from Italia '90, a pair of fake breasts strapped to his front while riding in an open-top bus, is unlike any you would normally associate with a professional footballer. It was one in a string of antics that caused Sir Bobby Robson to famously comment that his not-so-secret weapon was 'daft as a brush' – words doused in fatherly affection.

Quite recently when I was on holiday in Dubai with my wife, we were sitting down to dinner at a Chinese restaurant in the hotel when that loveable Geordie accent came into earshot. He made his way over to our table to have a chat, friendly and most polite as he always is, before insisting that he pay for our meal. Of course I declined, though it was very kind of him to offer, and after a few more words we parted ways. I thought nothing more of it until the following morning when I was talking to the hotel staff. They relayed to us the previous night's events, saying: 'Around 1.00 or 2.00 in the morning we had a bit of fun with Paul Gascoigne. He was walking around the hotel with a lobster in his hand which he'd nicked from the kitchen.' Some things never change!

Paul Gascoigne played the game in a way that just made you want to watch. You couldn't take your eyes off him because you knew if you did you might miss a spark of genius, or sometimes of lunacy. He showed a capability beyond that of any English midfielder of his generation, a naturally gifted talent who brought something completely different to the team. We've had great midfielders in England, but it's rare to find one outside of Brazil who is so adept at the art of dribbling. Many have mused over whether a move to Manchester United early in his career might have provided the necessary structure and discipline to prolong his time at the top, but there's no guarantee that he would have continued to be such an iridescent force if he'd been in the care of Sir Alex Ferguson. It does no good to ponder the ifs and maybes of Paul Gascoigne's career; instead let's celebrate it for what it was – an irreplaceable episode in English footballing history.

36. FRANCO BARESI

Having begun my days at West Ham as a bustling midfielder, once Ron Greenwood had spotted the centre forward in me there was absolutely no looking back. I spent my career battling with defenders, trying to outwit or outrun them, and as a result I gained a great deal of respect for those who dedicated their career to marking the likes of me out of games.

My old England teammate, big Jack Charlton, was a dab hand at this. We called him 'the Giraffe' due to his size and rather ungainly gait but the effectiveness of his methods could not be disputed. The concentration required to maintain focus, not letting your man out of reach or sight for 90 minutes, is something to be admired and was often a thankless task. Those around him would not have been able to play quite so freely without Jack doing the dirty work beside them, liberating them from defensive duties. I would be the first to sing Jack's praises as an integral part of our side in '66 but, purely on stylistic grounds, I've omitted him from my list along with countless other man-markers and no-nonsense stoppers.

I have however found space for the more adventurous defenders who played alongside people like Jack, those who were as comfortable with the ball at their feet as they were forcefully taking it from someone else's. There are few players in history who have fitted this description more aptly than Franco Baresi. Hear his name and you're immediately put in mind of the great defensive traditions of Italian football.

Baresi played in a position which is now largely defunct but one which was pivotal to so many sides throughout the 1970s and 80s, particularly on the Continent. The Italians elegantly referred to it as the libero role, which translates as 'free'. The English, practical and forthright as we are in our outlook, named it after its likeness to a broom. With the centre backs ahead of them pinned into position, the sweeper would sit deep, breaking up play and embarking on marauding runs or spraying passes to those ahead of them. They represented the last line of defence and the first stage of the attack, advancing rapidly to release the forwards.

It was a position that required great vision and an ability to read the game; Baresi had both in abundance. He studied the game as a youth team player at AC Milan's famed Milanello training complex, embracing the near-forensic approach his countrymen applied to the tactics of the game. Nils Liedholm, the coach who granted him his debut in 1978, said that 'at 18 he already had the knowledge of a veteran.' Within a year he had made the position his own and by the age of 22 he was captaining a new-look Milan side as they looked to rebuild, thriving under the expectations and pressure.

With the Italian national side, despite often being played out of position, which resulted in him refusing to take part in the '86 World Cup, he amassed 81 caps and always looked assured even against the very best. He collected a World Cup winner's medal in '82 but as an entirely unused substitute. Upon his return to international football he led Italy to the semi-finals of Euro '88 and Italia '90, but his most heroic turn came four years later in the World Cup in the USA.

Against Norway in Italy's second group game Baresi sustained a knee injury that required immediate surgery. For most players this would have signalled the end of their World Cup, but Franco wasn't most players. Just three weeks later he returned to his position in the starting line-up as Italy faced Brazil in the final. Tasked with handling Romário (the eventual Golden Ball winner) and his strike partner

Bebeto, there was no room for error. Thankfully for Baresi, he too had a capable partner in the form of a youthful Paolo Maldini, and the pair put in a flawless performance, frustrating the Brazilians for 120 minutes.

It was a phenomenal return from injury but the cruellest of blows was to follow. Having crashed out of the 1990 World Cup on penalties the Italians looked concerned as another tense shootout loomed. The nerves told as Baresi struck the first penalty high over the bar before another of Italy's stars of the tournament, Roberto Di Baggio, did exactly the same to hand victory to Brazil.

The disappointment of 1994 aside, his twenty-year career with Milan was littered with silverware as the club conquered all. The club were crowned champions of Europe on three occasions and won six Italian titles during his stay. They asserted themselves as one of club football's greatest ever sides with Franco Baresi's famous number 6 shirt being retired at the end of his career, presumably to the great relief of all future Milan defenders. Filling his shoes was a big enough ask without adding that iconic shirt to the mix.

35. STEVEN GERRARD

It seems strange to think of Steven Gerrard as one of the veterans of the English game but that's exactly what he is. Looking back on his career, although he might be disappointed not to have won a league title or challenged for honours with England, his is a story of many great successes.

A real all-rounder, his leadership and well-channelled

aggression are facets of his game that should be valued as highly as any of his technical traits. For a club like Liverpool, so accustomed to winning league titles, a lean period is always going to be hard to cope with but in Gerrard the fans found someone who made every game worth watching. He also played a commanding role in ensuring that it was less lean than it might otherwise have been, with some virtuoso performances as he dragged his side to glory.

The list of choices for his greatest game highlights just how often he has proved to be the difference between victory and defeat, winning silverware where a runners-up medal looked certain. As is now part of footballing folklore, throughout the 2004/05 season Gerrard continually and spectacularly drove Liverpool on to Champions League glory, despite them possessing a massively unfancied squad.

His goal to kick-start the most remarkable comeback from 3-0 down in the final vs. AC Milan and his tub-thumping celebration showed a captain with the ability to inspire and lead, but in the final group game he showed his talents as an individual. Facing Olympiakos at Anfield and requiring victory by a two-goal margin, the task looked achievable at the outset. However, with five minutes remaining and Liverpool still needing one more goal, they were on the brink of heading out with rumours that failure to progress would see Gerrard leave the club in search of trophies. But Gerrard wasn't prepared to give up without a fight, sending a half-volley crashing into the net with the outside of his right boot.

The dramatic climax to the 2004/05 season was undoubtedly the standout moment in his career but his performance in the FA Cup final against West Ham a year later was arguably more impressive, though I can't say I was pleased to witness it at the time. As a topsy-turvy game entered injury time, West Ham led 3-2 and Gerrard looked

to have finally been beaten. But once again, Liverpool's captain was about to show exactly why you should never write him off. With the ball falling to him more than 40 yards from goal, the strike that followed ranks among the best ever scored in an FA Cup final, as Liverpool went on to win in the penalty shootout.

It's a testament to Gerrard's focus that so many of these storybook moments have occurred throughout his career, with him refusing to give up even when the deficit appears insurmountable. It's also why he has endeared himself to fans of other clubs, who admire him for his loyalty and dedication, something that's coveted by the fans of any club. The fact that a much-mooted move to Chelsea never materialised was much to his benefit, as he has remained a vital part of his boyhood club. His continued presence in Liverpool's midfield, albeit in an altered role, has demonstrated his footballing intelligence as well.

Sadly, Gerrard's international career was a different matter altogether. One of those unhelpfully dubbed England's 'Golden Generation', he suffered from unfeasibly high expectations. Despite the underachievement of the side as a whole, when he retired from football in July 2014 he did so with great credit. Given the thankless task of captaining an England that could at best be described as a developing side at the 2014 World Cup, it was far from the glorious end he had hoped for but as was the case at Liverpool he took pride in helping to bring through a new generation.

Gerrard has simultaneously been one of the most dependable and unpredictable players to grace the Premier League, providing some of the competition's most memorable moments. With Liverpool seemingly on the brink of a bright new era, he has remained a constant source of hope and pride during a largely barren period.

No player goes through their career without drawing criticism and Gerrard was on the receiving end when Sir Alex Ferguson published his autobiography. The Scot claimed (perhaps mischievously) that he had never been 'a top, top player'. Nevertheless, few agreed with him and the outcry of support for Gerrard was telling. The words of Zinedine Zidane in particular seemed a far more accurate description. 'To say he is not a top player is wrong,' said Zidane, 'for two or three years, Steven Gerrard was the best midfield player in the world.' As a seal of approval from one of the greatest midfielders in history, one couldn't hope for better endorsement.

34. YAYA TOURÉ

When Yaya Touré arrived in England he did so with little ceremony. Despite a £24 million price tag, he had never really settled anywhere before. Brief stays in Ukraine, Greece and Monaco came before his arrival at Barcelona where he played a significant understudy role, operating in the shadows of Xavi, Iniesta and Messi. The phrase 'surplus to requirements' was the opinion held by the Spanish giants when he came to leave in 2010. Since then, he has grown immeasurably as a player, given the platform to perform in a star-studded Manchester City side. Admittedly, it also took City a little while to realise just how big a player he could be.

As part of the Barcelona side that won every trophy going, the Ivorian came with a pedigree for success. It was hoped that he could bring experience, particularly of European

competition, to City's midfield. Switching roles from game to game, he invariably shone brightest when given licence to attack, most memorably with a match-winning goal in the FA Cup semi-final against bitter rivals Manchester United – a feat he repeated in the final a month later against Stoke City.

These glimpses of creativity continued to provide standout moments over the course of the next two seasons, averaging nine goals a season as he juggled his defensive responsibilities. His attacking performances drew ever-increasing praise, but with Sergio Agüero, Edin Džeko and Carlos Tevez supplying the firepower up front his talents were in greater demand as a shield for the back four.

In May 2013 Manuel Pellegrini took over from Roberto Mancini at the City of Manchester Stadium and all was set to change for Touré. Four goals in the first six league games followed as his 2013/14 campaign got off to an explosive start. The same could be said of the team as a whole, with Man City regularly thrashing opponents when previously they would have sat on a one- or two-goal lead. He had bypassed his previous record league goals total by early December, scoring his 6th and 7th of the season in a 3-2 win over West Bromwich Albion.

Touré's form continued throughout the season and he once again showed himself to be a big game player at Wembley in the final of the League Cup against Sunderland. City fell behind to an early goal from Fabio Borini and began to fear a repeat of the FA Cup final the previous season, when they lost to a heavily unfancied Wigan side that got relegated three days later. This time around the Ivory Coast international stepped up, intervening with a sublime curled equaliser from outside the box. With Sunderland appearing to have covered all bases, Touré swept his foot through the ball sending it looping in over Vito Mannone in the Sunderland goal. The goal turned the tide and sent City on their way to their first trophy of the season.

It was in the final weeks of the Premier League season that his influence became more evident than ever. With the title seemingly in Liverpool's hands just three games from the end of the season, Touré provided a driving force in midfield and pushed the team on when it would have been easier to surrender. Of course, Touré's persistence paid off when a hugely unfortunate slip from Gerrard saw Liverpool fall to defeat against Chelsea and hand the advantage in the title race to Manchester City.

Yaya Touré is a player who has the ability to do the spectacular. Even with a considerable career behind him, the comparisons to Patrick Vieira that accompanied his signing for Manchester City seemed like a tall order but Touré has made them look conservative at best. While descriptions such as 'athletic box-to-box midfielder' or 'midfield powerhouse' are befitting of a player whose stamina, strength and power undeniably set him apart from the competition, these don't seem to do justice to his creativity and finesse.

The most likeable facet of Touré's game is that he defies comparison. He does display the same rangy gait that made Vieira such a spectacle, but he also has the passing range and vision of Steven Gerrard and the defensive positioning of Claude Makélélé. He seems to possess a little bit of all of the great midfielders in Premier League history and while I wouldn't dream of talking disparagingly of Barcelona's midfield, there really is no substitute for those lung-busting runs from one goalmouth to the other. With many of the world's star talents choosing La Liga over the Premier League, Touré is one player I'm delighted that we as a nation have inherited.

30=. ERIC CANTONA; DENNIS BERGKAMP; GIANFRANCO ZOLA; THIERRY HENRY

The Premier League as it stands today is completely unrecognisable compared to the First Division football I experienced during my playing days. The 1990s saw an influx of overseas talent and while some fear that this has stunted the technical growth of English players in recent years, I think the first wave of imports had a very positive effect.

These additions had an impact at all levels, with new tactical and mental approaches recognisable both on and off the pitch. Teams lower down the divisions were often able to recruit players of a far better standard than they would be restricted to in this country, with global scouting networks yet to take over. Cult heroes were made in their dozens, with surprising culture-clashes blossoming into long-lasting allegiances.

Of all the success stories of this internationalisation of our leagues, four signings stand out above all others. Four players who enjoyed great success with their respective clubs and whose names are still sung on the terraces even today – not to mention the odd statue being sculpted in their image!

Starting even before the Premier League came into existence, a Frenchman's tumultuous trial with Sheffield Wednesday proved to be the starting point for a glorious love affair with the English game. Following a promising first week with the South Yorkshire club, Eric Cantona was less than impressed when Trevor Francis asked him to stay on for an extra week's trial just so that they could make certain. Of course, his answer was 'non!', but he was keen to stay on in England due to a lack of appreciation back home.

Wednesday's loss was Leeds United's gain, albeit briefly, with their Yorkshire rivals signing him up. Joining a team powered by the momentum of a promotion the summer before and going strong in the First Division, Cantona settled immediately. His class was plain to see and he quickly became an important figure in Leeds' attack, operating in a supporting role behind the prolific Lee Chapman. A league title at the first time of asking was vindication of his decision to leave France, but he was about to repeat his habit of crossing enemy lines.

After an eye-catching year, he departed for a team on the other side of the Pennines, beginning his historic association with Manchester United. Signing in late 1992 for a bargain fee of £1.2 million, he sparked a turnaround that ultimately propelled a faltering United side to a league championship – their first since 1967. As he had at Leeds, Cantona brought out the best in his teammates with great composure and a fantastic ability to pick a pass.

It was the following season, however, that saw Cantona become the main event at Old Trafford. Improving upon his impressive start in English football, he began to add goals to his game as Manchester United's reign of dominance began to gather pace. During his five-year stay at the club, Cantona amassed four league titles and two FA Cups to add to the old First Division title he'd won at Leeds. His technical ability was of the highest standard and he often left fans cooing in awe with some of his more audacious attempts, including a lobbed goal from outside the area against Sunderland.

These goals got the headlines and deservedly so, but even once he'd become the undisputed King of Old Trafford, his team play continued to impress me. With many a defence distracted by the star man, he regularly used his almost magnetic pull to drag players out of position allowing his teammates to capitalise. It might not be the most exciting of skills but it's the sort of ability that wins games.

Unquestionably keen to replicate Cantona's success story, in 1995 Arsenal looked to Italy for their foreign talisman. Arsenal followed Sir Alex Ferguson's approach to recruitment, targeting an individual with a slightly more proven track record than the one Sheffield Wednesday and Leeds had gambled on. Having already proven his worth at Ajax before joining Inter Milan, Dennis Bergkamp was already a world-class player – Arsenal's first overseas recruit to fit such a description.

Though they were of a similar standard, Bergkamp and Cantona were very different personalities. Cantona was a confident, swaggering and sometimes brooding character, whereas Bergkamp looked almost shy at times. This was reflected in his comparatively slow start as he struggled to adapt to Arsenal's archetypally English set-up. All that was set to change a year into the Dutch international's stay. As Bruce Rioch made way for France's Arsène Wenger, a surprise recruitment from Japan, Arsenal took their first brave steps towards modernisation.

Bringing with him a far more professional regime, Wenger's style suited Bergkamp perfectly. He grew in confidence and importance constantly until in 1997/98 he helped Arsenal to a league and cup double. His gradual growth and integration was an important part of not only his progression but that of the team as a whole. With Wenger methodically overhauling the approach of the club, the team came to fit around Bergkamp which was a recipe for success.

The Dutchman's ability to improve those around him was even greater than Cantona's and he remained a constant in a side that saw players such as Marc Overmars, Emmanuel

Petit and Nicolas Anelka depart for Spain in big-money deals. I expect that, had you asked him at the time, Arsène Wenger wouldn't have needed to think twice about which player he most wanted to retain.

One team that has called upon foreign talent more than most is Chelsea, a tendency which began over the course of one summer in particular. With legendary Dutchman Ruud Gullit their player-manager, they made three noteworthy foreign signings in June 1996. Two of these were Italian – Roberto Di Matteo and Gianluca Vialli (another future player-manager) – along with France's Frank Leboeuf. Enthused by their strong start to life at Chelsea, Gullit was soon back in the market. His fourth signing that year was to top the lot.

Signing from Parma, Gianfranco Zola like Cantona wasn't valued all that highly in his home nation but settled very well over here, enjoying the fast-paced football that set us apart. He had a penchant for the spectacular and delighted in showing this off. The more frenetic style of play enabled him to display his quick-thinking creativity, scoring from the most outrageous of positions. Though he undoubtedly had the ability to unlock the stern defences of Italy, the chance to wreak havoc on the slightly less organised English equivalents was far more to his liking.

He had all the physical hallmarks of his fellow former Neapolitan, Diego Maradona, particularly in terms of height and hair. While these features came naturally, he worked tirelessly to develop many more of Maradona's traits: 'I learned everything from Diego. I used to spy on him every time he trained and learned how to curl a free-kick just like him.' When he was in full flow, there were definite glimpses of Maradona in his play.

Though Zola's time in England didn't yield the league

titles that Cantona or Bergkamp's did, he enjoyed success in cup competitions, winning two FA Cups, a League Cup and a Cup Winners' Cup in his time. While, on paper, his time may not have been quite as successful as that of his peers, Zola's impact was far more profound as a result. In a team that had talent but ultimately fell short of the standards of their London and Manchester rivals, Zola brought sheer delight to the fans on a weekly basis. Whereas Cantona spearheaded a formidable attack, and Bergkamp pulled the strings for a phenomenally fluid Arsenal side, Zola was the unpredictable showman in a hit-and-miss side.

Three years after Zola's arrival in England, four after Bergkamp's and two after Cantona's retirement, Arsène Wenger made a foreign signing that even their legacies didn't seem to justify. Signing for £11 million after just sixteen ineffectual games for Juventus and seen as a direct replacement for top scorer Nicolas Anelka, Thierry Henry was a signing that prompted an awful lot of head scratching. The cranial itching grew no less prominent once fans got a chance to see him in action, as he failed to find the net in his first seven games. He had played as a left winger in Italy but Wenger was adamant that Henry's future lay up front, convinced by a brief period as his coach in the French youth set-up. He tried to explain his confidence to the doubting public, saying, 'He was the top scorer in the under-17s for France when I first had him and I think that, as well as having the qualities of youth, pace and power, he is a good finisher.'

In Arsenal's eighth game of the season Henry finally broke his duck with a winner away at Southampton, but it was not until late November that he finally began to score with any regularity. From then on, the games in which Henry failed to score became the rarity, finishing what had once looked

like a doomed first season with 26 goals. In a team that already boasted Dennis Bergkamp, Davor Šuker and Marc Overmars, he had managed to shine.

Thierry Henry was not only a new breed of foreign import – a young player with potential, as opposed to an experienced pro looking for a change – he was also a completely different prospect to Bergkamp, Cantona or Zola. Henry's primary asset was his unrivalled pace, but this was made lethal by his ability to act and react when in full flow. Within a year of signing he seemed to do all the things Anelka had once dazzled Highbury with, but somehow better and without the attitude. After a year or two more it became almost accepted that Ian Wright's goal-scoring record was going to be beaten. Once in motion, Thierry Henry powered through his Arsenal career in the same unstoppable fashion that he tore through helpless defences, becoming one of the most prolific foreign talents ever to grace our shores.

Now, with the England national team continuing to founder, the blame is directed at the international nature of the Premier League. Players of the calibre of Cantona and Zola, Henry and Bergkamp have done more for our game than most Englishmen, however. The chance to see such mercurial talents on a weekly basis, and for home-grown players to play alongside them, is invaluable and no league in the world would, or at least should, turn their ilk away.

Striking the right balance between home-grown and overseas talent is always important, though. Spain and Germany have got this right in recent years, promoting their own players where possible but embracing foreign talent all the same. We shouldn't be so down on our own youngsters as to suggest that they couldn't teach players from other nations a thing or two. Southampton have supplied a fantastic blueprint in recent years, but the exodus of their

British stars and their continued production line only goes to show how far ahead of the rest they remain.

Luke Shaw in particular has all the ability to be a great player in world football, but this requires patience. For all the media furore that surrounded his time off the pitch in England, Ashley Cole's footballing career was almost exemplary in this regard. He racked up cap after cap and many people seemed to be taken by surprise when he made his 100th England appearance, yet very few would argue that it wasn't deserved. If we are to produce another Ashley Cole, or even a Bergkamp or a Cantona, then we will need to have patience and realise that our own players might need as much time to settle in our leagues as these sparkling imports.

29. SIR TOM FINNEY

When Sir Tom Finney passed away in February 2014, the clamour from the wider footballing world to pay respect was overwhelming. He's a player that the majority are too young to have seen on the pitch and he was never one to court fame. Nevertheless, his death was marked with the sort of ceremony rarely seen in the modern game.

Thousands lined the streets as the funeral procession passed through Preston to a chorus of applause en route to Preston Minster. While hundreds attended the official ceremony, Preston North End's Deepdale ground was filled with mourners who had gathered to view the service on the stadium's big screen. Football fans are a loyal bunch and like to remember their own, but this went beyond the normal

displays of respect. Finney was the last of a bygone era, a player who is best remembered in still images and black-and-white footage.

One such image came in 1956 at Stamford Bridge in a match between Preston and Chelsea. Following torrential rain prior to the game, the pitch had been left in a sodden state and Finney said in later years: 'The match would not have been played today because there were huge pools of water on the playing surface.' As he battled with the elements on the right wing to control a pass from Tommy Docherty, his feet slipped beneath him sending up a great spray of water. The photograph of this moment, Finney partly obscured by the mist, won the Sports Photograph of the Year in 1956 and in 2004 Preston commissioned a sculpture of it outside Deepdale.

While most statues depict a player with fists clenched in victory, or striking a winning goal, this snapshot was quintessentially Finney. Even in proper football boots, the pitch beneath was too moveable for traction and still he recovered to swing a dangerous cross into the box. It's football as a sport, rather than a business. What's more, for the man they called the Preston Plumber after the part-time job he worked at alongside his playing career, what better way to commemorate his life than with a fully-functioning fountain?

He was so ingrained in Preston North End that the season after he retired the club were relegated and have never since returned. Yet while Preston struggled to cope without Finney, he proved with the England national team that he could excel in different surroundings. He scored 30 times in 76, including goals in his debuts as an outside left, outside right and centre forward, showing him to be one of the most versatile and talented attackers of his generation. In May of 1950 Finney travelled to Portugal with an England team containing Stan Mortensen, Wilf Mannion, Jackie Milburn and even a veteran Sir Alf Ramsey. The game was only a friendly but saw Finney score his only international hat-trick as England ran out victors in a 5-3 win.

Despite impressing on the Continent, Preston chairman Nat Buck made sure that he would remain on English soil. When Palermo of Italy expressed their interest in signing Finney in 1952, a move that would have brought Finney great riches, Buck intervened, saying: 'You can forget all about that, if tha' doesn't play for us, tha' doesn't play for anybody.' Finney had little say in the matter but in later years expressed his gratitude at the decision, claiming that he might not be so widely revered throughout the town (now a city) had he moved on when he had the chance.

Finney's prioritisation of the views of the fans over the contents of his own pocket show the quality of the man. He realised his value to the community, although he was always too modest to admit it, because he was part of the community. He would walk to home matches alongside those who adored him and continued to bang the drum for Preston years after his retirement. By all accounts he never really got used to people calling him Sir after his knighthood in 1998, but the locals would doubtless have called him Sir Tom whether he'd been knighted or not.

It's rare in this day and age to have such a tangible link to the past and so when Sir Tom Finney passed away it felt as though the golden era of football had slipped that little bit further away too. One thing's for sure though: the local boy who went on to be one of the world's greatest will never slip away from Preston North End.

28. PETER SCHMEICHEL

It's often said that goalkeepers are mad and to be honest, if they are it's hard to blame them. Left alone at the back of the pitch and only really noticed when they're making mistakes, it can be a pretty lonely existence at times. So when a goalkeeper comes along and suddenly becomes the centre of attention, people are bound to take note. That was the case when Denmark's Peter Schmeichel signed for Manchester United in 1991.

Now we'd all seen Colombia's René Higuita grabbing the headlines for reasons other than goalkeeping; his tendency to push up to the halfway line gained notoriety, while his 'scorpion kick' clearance caught the eye. Yet Schmeichel managed to get noticed for far more productive and worthwhile reasons. Admittedly one of them was the imposing Dane's ability to be heard over even the loudest of crowds, but he wasn't just yelling for the sake of it. He was a new breed of goalkeeper who wasn't content just standing behind the defence, he practically controlled them.

With his first league season ending in disappointment, winning the League Cup in April but narrowly missing out on the title to rivals Leeds United, the summer months held some unexpected glory. After initially failing to qualify for UEFA Euro '92 in Sweden, Denmark were drafted in as a late replacement for the expelled Yugoslavs.

Over the course of the next month the footballing world looked on in astonishment as Schmeichel and co. rode the wave of momentum all the way. Favouring a rear-guard approach, Brian Laudrup was their undisputed star name after his brother refused to cancel his holiday to join up

with the team, but Henrik Larsen (not to be confused with Sweden's Henrik Larsson), John Jensen and Kim Vilfort made names for themselves en route to victory.

Schmeichel saved from Marco Van Basten in a semi-final penalty shootout against the Netherlands to qualify for the final where they faced heavy favourites Germany. The odds were emphatically defied as Denmark won 2-0 in one of the most memorable finals in European Championships history. Schmeichel was named as the goalkeeper in UEFA's Team of the Tournament and he returned to England a cult hero.

1992/93 saw the dawn of a new era in English football with the inaugural Premier League season. On the face of it, this was a basic rebranding of the old First Division, but with big-money television deals in place the riches that accompanied success promised to be game-changing. The birth of the Premier League was accompanied by one small but significant rule change – the outlawing of the back-pass.

No longer could defenders roll the ball back for the keeper to collect when they came under the slightest bit of pressure. No longer would games be closed out by the goalkeeper and centre half playing keep-ball. A new age of frantic defending had arrived and it required an ultra-organised defensive unit, including a goalkeeper, to cope. Schmeichel's performances in Sweden that summer had come at an opportune moment as, with his reputation enhanced, he was able to command a defence that included such seasoned pros as Gary Pallister and Steve Bruce with far greater authority.

The silverware soon followed as Manchester United were crowned champions in five of the next seven league seasons, including an unprecedented League, FA Cup and Champions League-winning treble season in 1998/99. Schmeichel grew into one of the greatest shot-stoppers in world football, particularly lauded for his ability in one-on-one situations.

With the club growing into the dominant force in English football during his stay, it remained unclear how they would cope when he left for Portugal in the summer of 1999. They had formed one of the meanest defensive units in the league and the man they called the Great Dane was not easy to replace. Six seasons and a whole host of faltering replacements, including Fabien Barthez, Massimo Taibi and Tim Howard, failed to make the grade before Edwin Van Der Sar finally met the required standards in 2005.

Even today, with David De Gea who took more than a season to settle at the club, the shadow of Peter Schmeichel looms large at Old Trafford and it is clear to see why. His list of individual achievements reveals how he managed to transcend the old role of the goalkeeper, never in danger of becoming the forgotten man between the sticks. Voted the Premier League Player of the Season for his performances in 1995/96, he remains the only goalkeeper to have won the award since its introduction the season before. To get noticed as a goalkeeper is one thing, but to be acclaimed is another matter entirely.

27. LOTHAR MATTHÄUS

Lothar Matthäus was a footballing colossus, competing and excelling at the top level for two decades. He became a fixture of a Bayern Munich side that won seven Bundesliga titles during his two spells with the club (1984–88 and 1992–2000), either side of a brief but successful period with Italy Internazionale in which he won Serie A and the UEFA Cup.

Barely a season went by when he wasn't seriously competing for honours and usually he ended up victorious.

More impressive still was his international career. With 150 caps he is Germany's most capped player, both in total and in terms of World Cup appearances (25). Operating as a box-to-box midfielder in his early days before developing into a holding midfielder and eventually a sweeper, his record of 23 goals is also very impressive. He is the only outfield player in history to have competed in five World Cups and he captained his side to the title in 1990, having picked up a runners-up medal in '82 and '86. Add to this his European Championship winner's medal from 1980 and you begin to understand the magnitude of this natural and unrelenting challenger.

Having had the pleasure of meeting him, I can gladly say that he's a very likeable guy too. A sociable character with an interest in how everyone else is getting on, it's clear to see why he was such an effective captain. Yet for all this consistency, he was much, much more than merely a steady presence in the middle of the pitch. His performances often proved to be the difference between success and failure, as some of football's finest talents will attest.

As a player who played in both the European Cup and the Champions League and turned out for Germany and West Germany, he straddles two very different eras. He is an iconic figure to several generations and has shared the pitch with players we associate with completely differing times; from Felix Magath and Arie Haan, Maradona and Platini, right through to Xavi and Beckham.

His two famous duels with Diego Maradona alone seemed to encapsulate the transition between two great eras and led to the Argentine saying: 'He is the best rival I've ever had. I guess that's enough to define him.' In terms of World Cup finals the two finished up with one victory each, Maradona captaining Argentina to a 3-2 victory in '86 before Matthäus got revenge in 1990, leading West Germany to a 1-0 win. Tactical, skilful and hard-fought affairs, the matchups provided the most enjoyable of spectacles – two great players in opposing positions facing up against one another. Like Charlton and Beckenbauer in '66, and later Beckenbauer and Cruyff in '74, these moments are rare and to be savoured.

Maradona's comments weren't just lip service either. When Matthäus finally retired from the game in 2000, a testimonial was held to commemorate a glittering career for club and country, rather fittingly pitting one against the other as Bayern took on Germany. Obviously never having played for either, Diego Maradona's presence as the guest of honour signified the depth of respect he had for the German. Not least because his appearance came shortly after treatment for a life-threatening heart disease.

There are so many reasons to admire Lothar Matthäus and his career. His personal achievements at international level are astounding, as is the trophy haul he was instrumental in winning. There's also the small matter of being voted both European and World Player of the Year in the early 1990s. But beyond all of his quantifiable accolades, the markers by which most budding professionals will wish to measure their success, it's the warmth of feeling with which the footballing world regards him that I find most admirable. To win is one thing, but to do so in the right way is far, far harder and is pivotal to the respect he has garnered. And if you're still not convinced, just take a look at all of the great German players he outperformed and outlasted.

24=. CARLOS ALBERTO TORRES; ROBERTO RIVELINO; JAIRZINHO (Jair Ventura Filho)

In any discussion of the footballing greats it is inevitable that you will spend a fair amount of time talking about Brazilians, and in any discussion of Brazilian football it's difficult to leave out the great side of the '70s. As much as I was tempted to include the entire England squad from 1966 in my 50, I could have done exactly the same with Brazil's Seleção from 1970.

It was the rarest of things, a great team packed full of great individuals, each capable of giving a star turn. Of course they boasted the brightest of jewels in their crown – the great Pelé – but they would have been a force even without him.

Theirs are names familiar to football fans the world over, fixed in the memory as the soundtrack to so many beautiful flowing moves as commentators reeled off the name of player after iconic player. Carlos Alberto, Rivelino, Jairzinho are the three I've selected in joint 24th place, but Tostão, Clodoaldo and Gérson were equally vital to their success.

Even with the controversy surrounding Bobby Moore and our defeat at the hands of West Germany, the World Cup in Mexico in 1970 was a thoroughly enjoyable experience. So much so that I vowed to return if the tournament were ever held there again and stayed true to my word, flying out to enjoy it all over again in 1986.

As the first World Cup to be broadcast in colour, it represented a new era of watching football. Fans at home were able to see Brazil's bright yellow shirts, England's sky blue shorts and the light green of the sun-bleached pitches

of Mexico. It made for a far more attractive spectacle with the ball no longer getting lost amid the greyscale images.

For Brazil, everything fell into place. Their kits would dazzle television audiences and the South American climate suited them more than most. Though not known for certain at the time, it would be Pelé's final World Cup and Brazil's heavyweights would star in some of the most oft-repeated television footage in finals history. They also had an incentive that no other team shared. Having already won the competition twice before, in 1958 and 1962, a third triumph would see them keep the trophy.

Managed by Mario Zagallo, a flying winger who had won the World Cup as a player in '58 and '62, the side was built in his own attack-minded image. Gérson orchestrated from the centre of midfield, controlling the play and creating openings with a magnificent range of passes. He was by no means a defensive player but has been remembered as such simply because of his withdrawn position and the all-out attacking nature of those ahead of him. At times his style of play seemed far more befitting of an Englishman than a man who spent his entire career in Brazil, and I mean that as a big compliment.

With Carlos Alberto and Everaldo flanking him, Gérson's positional discipline while playmaking was vital in maintaining the side's shape. Along with Brito and Wilson Piazza at centre back, left back Everaldo has also been forgotten somewhat over time, overshadowed by the more memorable names from the side, but all three could play. Further to that, despite Carlos Alberto's attacking prowess his defensive work should not be overlooked.

This solid base was completed by the holding midfielder Clodoaldo. Like Gérson, he was a defensive midfielder by Brazilian definition alone. For most of the 1970 tournament he dropped slightly deeper than Gérson, providing defensive cover while his teammate played his creative part. Yet when the two switched roles against Uruguay in the semi-final, with the Brazilians trailing by a goal to nil and struggling to force a breakthrough, Clodoaldo proved that he was just as effective in attack.

Having recognised the underrated and overlooked stars of the team, we come to four of the most heralded players in history. In Tostão, Jairzinho, Rivelino and Pelé, Zagallo squeezed so much attacking talent into his front four that it was almost cruel on defences.

Tostão was a supremely intelligent individual. Though he finished the tournament with two goals to his name, he was at times utterly selfless. 'I was an attacking midfielder,' he explained after the tournament, 'serving as a linchpin and supporting the superstars that came behind me.' Not to be confused with the more industrious hold-up men of the day, his approach was that of a cultured schemer. His inclusion was in serious doubt as he had been recovering from a detached retina, but Tostão's vision was better than anyone's in 1970, picking out impossible-looking passes to set up goals and opportunities.

The three who played off him were almost impossible to track. Pelé attacked through the middle from deep with Rivelino cutting in from the left and Jairzinho from the right (not to mention Carlos Alberto on the overlap). At times it seemed like they had too many players on the pitch as defences struggled to delegate marking duties. The movement was devastatingly effective.

Roberto Rivelino was a joy to watch down the left wing. He always exerted such perfect control over the ball, whether he was dribbling at pace, shooting or picking out a teammate, or outwitting goalkeepers with ferocious swerving shots.

With his prominent moustache he often looked like a mad professor performing outrageous experiments on the ball. He finished the tournament with three goals including a hammer of a free-kick against Czechoslovakia.

Jairzinho on the opposite wing was much more direct than Rivelino, which led to the nickname of Furacão da Copa, the World Cup Hurricane. His standout achievement in that tournament was the envy of every attacking player in the game, except Uruguay's Alcides Ghiggia. The two share the enviable honour of being the only men in World Cup history to score in every match of a tournament, including the final. Just Fontaine came close in 1958, but defeat to Brazil in the semi-final meant that he had to settle for a watered-down version, replacing the final with four goals in the third place playoff.

That leaves Pelé who was his sensational self. With so much firepower emanating from all over the pitch, it was impossible to focus solely on marking Pelé as many teams would have liked. Of course he turned provider for one of Jairzinho's seven strikes that summer, defeating England and boosting Brazilian confidence like no other goal could have. We had fought hard to remain the dominant side in world football but Brazil were worthy successors.

The victory enabled Brazil to top our group with maximum points and secure the easier quarter-final fixture, coming up against Peru while we crashed out to West Germany. A fairly routine 4-2 victory saw Brazil progress to the semi-finals, where they faced a far bigger obstacle. With a chance to put an end to two decades of mourning, the opponents were Uruguay, the team who had humiliated them on home soil in the 1950 final. Even today the 2-1 defeat at the Maracanã is a sore subject in the country.

When Uruguay took the lead around the twenty-minute

mark with an awkward hooked shot which wrong-footed Félix in goal, there were fears of a repeat. The decision to give Clodoaldo more attacking licence provided an unlikely hero who scored a wonderful equaliser with the outside of his boot shortly before half-time to settle nerves and give the Seleção fifteen minutes to plot their attack from a level footing. Jairzinho gave Brazil the lead with a quarter of an hour remaining, a goal that seemed almost inevitable. Bearing down on the keeper following a fluid counter-attack, he never looked like missing. With fewer than twenty seconds of normal time left, Rivelino added a thumping third as Brazil claimed their place in the final.

In the other semi-final, Italy required extra time to over-come West Germany by four goals to three. The Italians were a strong outfit too, with notable names such as Sandro Mazzola, Roberto Boninsegna and Angelo Domenghini, considered big players in the European game, not to mention Luigi Riva who remains the nation's all-time top scorer to this day.

The final began as a close-fought battle too, with Bonin-segna cancelling out Pelé's earlier header with ten minutes of the first half remaining, following some calamitous play from the Brazilians in their own half. Brazil's superiority did however begin to tell as the second half wore on, as it had against Uruguay in the previous fixture. The wealth of attacking options gradually led to physical and mental exhaustion in their opposition. Brazil's gradual and systematic erosion of the Italian defensive wall was hugely significant, as Italy had been famed for their solidity in defence. If they couldn't shut out Zagallo's side, surely no one could.

Rivelino slammed a shot against the bar following a short free-kick before Gérson eventually regained the lead for Brazil, jinking past one challenge and striking from range as another flew towards him. It was a well-deserved goal, and not just for his performances in the tournament as a whole, as he had been the standout man for Brazil in a fierce tactical battle.

Five minutes later Gérson again showed his value, finding Pelé in the box with a pinpoint pass from the halfway line, which he headed down to set up Jairzinho for his obligatory goal. At 3-1 the game became an exhibition of Brazil's dominance. Pass after pass after pass followed as the game neared its conclusion, but they still found time for one further strike to round the game off in style; the goal to define an era in Brazilian football.

The move began deep in Brazil's half, with Clodoaldo, Pelé and Gérson playing the ball about in a triangle. Then Clodoaldo decided to have some fun, slaloming between four Italian defenders before laying the ball off to Rivelino. Much to their credit, the Italians refrained from scything him down as I'm sure they would have been sorely tempted to do. Rivelino looked up and found Jairzinho ahead of him with an effortless pass, the right winger moving over to the left in search of the action. Turning to face the weary defenders, Jairzinho shifted the ball on to his right foot and moved towards goal, playing the ball to Pelé's feet. Then for what felt like an age, Pelé did nothing. To all those watching on television they looked to have run out of options, but if the previous few weeks of football had taught us anything it was that Brazil never ran out of options.

And then he appeared, Brazil's captain and right back. With the most casual of passes, Pelé rolled the ball to the right into the path of Carlos Alberto for him to hammer in Brazil's fourth of the game and their nineteenth of the tournament. It was his one and only World Cup strike. I suppose if you're only going to score once you might as well make sure it's memorable.

Pelé came away from the World Cup in 1970 with the Golden Ball Award, an honour bestowed upon the tournament's standout player, but it was an award earned by the entire team. Rarely do you see so many talents converging in the same team, rarer still do they all hit their peak in a World Cup year. It's immensely difficult to select just three of the remaining ten to represent the team in my list. Gérson and Tostão would not have looked out of place in this list and Clodoaldo's performances in 1970 revealed him to be an invaluable team player, settling for a reduced role but shining when the opportunity came in the semi-final. I'm afraid Everaldo, Brito, Piazza and Félix's exclusion can be put down to my attacking bias.

I have always felt that if you were to add Pelé and Gérson to the three players I've selected here – Jairzinho, Rivelino and Carlos Alberto – then you would have the greatest five-a-side team in history, one worthy of giving most eleven-a-side outfits a run for their money. I'd even leave out a goalkeeper just to give the opposition a chance!

23. GORDON BANKS

England's greatest ever goalkeeper and Pelé's most famous nemesis, Gordon Banks was an easy choice for this list. I remember the first time I came up against him in training, just calmly and casually pinging shots at him in goal. Without the focus of a competitive match, usually these exercises see a few fly in but with Gordon this was never the case. Shot after shot was stopped, often with ease. It quickly became apparent that I had come across something special.

At first this was rather disconcerting – it's never nice as a striker to come up against an immovable object between the sticks – but he made sure you were pushed to your limits in each and every training session, a recipe for improvement. You knew that if you got the ball past Gordon, you could get the ball past anyone.

When most people think of Gordon Banks they think of that save against Pelé in the 1970 World Cup, which is understandable. It's only natural then that whenever people meet him the first thing they ask him about is that save and it always raises a smile to see him respond. Almost without fail, he'll give a withering sigh and mutter something along the lines of 'I'm fed up of people talking about that save, that's all they ever want to know about,' before quickly perking up and saying, 'but I'll talk you through it.' It's a story he loves telling and so he should.

During that tournament he was as good as I'd ever seen him, and was performing at a level that I'm not sure I've seen a keeper reach before or since. This was highlighted by the panic that surged through the team when he fell ill ahead of the 1970 quarter-final. Even with a perfectly able deputy in Peter Bonetti, the reaction of Sir Alf and coach Harold Shepherdson spoke volumes. With a knock-out fixture against West Germany fast approaching, the pair grew increasingly fearful of losing their number 1. So much so that, having initially insisted on conducting a pre-match fitness test, when the time came to carry it out, Shepherdson subjected him to the most timid of tests imaginable. An underhand roll of the ball was as stern as the task got, but it was plain to see that Gordon was in no fit state to stand up, let alone play, so he was left out with regret.

For all the plaudits Gordon received for his form that year, he has always maintained that his most important save was the one against me in the 1972 League Cup final, when we were playing for West Ham and Stoke City respectively. In the second leg of a tie that would eventually stretch to two additional replays, we won a penalty which I stepped up to take.

Scholar of the game that he was, Banksy knew my penalty routines and giveaways as well as I did, so when he saw me start my usual longish run-up he made the most educated of guesses that I'd strike it to his right. His confidence in his decision ensured that even though I hit it with some power, he moved early and was able to get right behind it to push it up and away. The save kept Stoke in the tie, as they eventually progressed with a 3-2 victory in the second replay before beating Chelsea 2-1 at Wembley. It may not have had the same global audience as the save from Pelé, but it ultimately led to silverware.

It's important to bear in mind that Banksy never had a goalkeeping coach. Essentially he taught himself how to play the game and I think that's what makes him such a special talent in my eyes. He had an ability to adapt his game in rather material ways, even during tournaments, if he felt it could improve his game. His instincts rarely failed him.

He perfected the art of positioning, creating angles that deprived strikers of gaps to aim for while ensuring that his reach was as broad as possible. His methodology didn't stop there either. When he started out, though it seems strange now, goalkeepers didn't wear gloves. Once he saw other keepers wearing them he was keen to try them out but, unlike other stoppers, he went one stage further.

Through some stroke of genius he realised that by rubbing chewing gum on his gloves he could achieve a better grip, making them more adhesive. He was so sure of his methods that one time, having turned up for a match only to realise

that the trainer had forgotten to pack the chewing gum, Gordon sent him off to the shops to pick some up for him. He wasn't being a prima donna, he just had so much belief in these little details and with his record you'd be foolish to question him.

I have to admit I thought long and hard about placing Gordon Banks much higher up this list. As the best goalkeeper I've ever played with or against, there's an argument for including him in the top ten but in truth I've just never been able to derive the same pleasure from seeing a great save as I do from witnessing a stunning goal. Call it the strikers' union or payback for that save in '72; either way it's my list!

22. LUIS FIGO

Before Cristiano Ronaldo there was Luis Figo, the Portuguese number 7 who worked his way up from Sporting Lisbon to Real Madrid via the Nou Camp, smashing transfer records along the way and creating the blueprint for his young successor's rise to fame.

Much like his eventual replacement for club and country, Figo played most of his football from out wide but was just as comfortable and effective in the middle of the field. He had the attributes to play in pretty much any attacking position, with unerringly potent dribbling, pinpoint crossing and an often match-winning shot just some of the weapons at his disposal.

Having asserted himself as Portuguese football's brightest star during his time with Sporting Lisbon, a move to a more prestigious league was long mooted so it came as little surprise when in 1995 he made the move to Barcelona. It was equally unsurprising that the step up was made so comfortably by Figo. He cemented his place in the first team almost immediately and was rewarded with a number of trophies during his five-year stay at the club, including a Cup Winners' Cup, two Copa del Rey victories and two league titles. Despite his success, what followed since has made him one of the most loathed personalities in Barcelona's history.

In the summer of 2000, a few hundred miles west of the Nou Camp, Real Madrid were plotting one of the most outrageous transfer bids in history. Meeting a buy-out clause in Figo's contract reported to be around the £37 million mark, they began talks with the star of the Catalonian side. Barcelona were powerless to resist as he signed a bumper deal, making the switch few believed would ever happen. It marked the start of a big-spending era for Real Madrid, as club president Florentino Pérez made clear his intention to secure one major signing each and every summer. He called these players Galácticos and the name stuck, for better or worse.

True to his word, Pérez followed up Figo's signature with that of Zinedine Zidane, David Beckham and Brazil's Ronaldo, to add to the considerable home-grown talent they already boasted in the shape of Raúl and Casillas. In a squad swelled with talent and egos, it would be easy for players to get lost among the crowd, but there was never any danger of that when it came to Figo.

Though it is undoubtedly easier to succeed when you're surrounded by the finest talents in world football, it takes a big player to stand out from the crowd and, if required, take on the responsibility when it's not going so well. This is exactly what Figo did – and what led to him being a near-permanent fixture in a side that was prone to rotation.

Midway through his first season with Real Madrid, Figo was awarded one of the most prestigious individual prizes in football – the Ballon d'Or, awarded to Europe's best player – and the following year he went one better, winning the World Player of the Year award. Yet like all great players, this personal recognition would have meant little had Madrid failed to perform as a team. La Liga wins in 2000/01 and 2002/03 and a Champions League win sandwiched in between ensured that Figo's time at Madrid was an unequivocal success.

He parted ways with Madrid and Spain in the summer of 2005, moving to Italy to join Inter Milan, where, after four consecutive title-winning seasons, he ended his career. It was a fitting end to a career filled with silverware. Known throughout the world as a classy professional of the highest order, I fear he's someone whose career we've come to take for granted.

Figo didn't have the unreliable edge that makes some lesser players more memorable. There was no short fuse to trip him up. He wasn't the type of player anyone ever accused of going missing, or failing to perform in the biggest games. Season after season he would impress while new pretenders would come and go. All highly desirable qualities and ones that have led me to include him in this list, but this is something that has perhaps come to count against him in the years since.

Playing at a time when style was often valued over sub-stance, and best known for his time at a club that was emblematic of this, he was an astoundingly well-rounded and reliable individual. It may not be headline-grabbing – though Figo often stole the show – but this consistency certainly deserves to be celebrated.

21. JOSEF MASOPUST

During my career I was fortunate enough to travel much of the world with club and country. On England duty I had the honour of a World Cup in Mexico and a friendly in the Maracanã in Brazil, and en route to Cup Winners' Cup glory with West Ham in '65 we visited Belgium, Czechoslovakia and Spain. Always a memorable experience, with far fewer televised matches there was an educational element too.

The styles and approaches from country to country, continent to continent, differed far more than they do today and at club level these trips often pitted us against great players whom most of the world knew nothing about. It's easy to forget that there was a time when entire clubs consisted of home-grown talent. I was to find out just how differently our great game could be played on a memorable trip to the USA.

In 1963 I travelled to the US with West Ham United to take part in a friendly tournament held annually in New York. It was a strange combination of nations, formats and titles and was funded by Bill Cox, owner of the Philadelphia Phillies baseball team. The competition was a forerunner to the North American Soccer League (which I later played in for the Seattle Sounders) and today's Major League Soccer, trying to bring the game to a potentially vast audience.

The majority of the tournament took place under the banner of the International Soccer League. It consisted of two groups or 'sections' comprising seven teams. Our group, Section I, included Recife of Brazil, Italy's Mantova and, from closer to home, Kilmarnock. It was the sort of opportunity you only really got if you qualified for the Cup Winners' Cup or were in the national team. Having only recently broken

into the England team, this was my first prolonged exposure to international football of any kind.

Despite making a slow start to the tournament we received a welcome boost ahead of the third match in the shape of Bobby Moore, returning from his duties with the national team to join up with us, and our fortunes soon began to turn.

At full strength, we topped the group and qualified for the championship game, the first of our two finals (bear with me). Poland's Górnik Zabrze were our opponents having won Section II, overcoming clubs such as Dinamo Zagreb (Yugoslavia, now Croatia) and Real Valladolid (Spain). We won 2-1 on aggregate and progressed to our next final, the grand final, to contest a one-game tournament called the American Challenge Cup (ACC).

Far from a run-of-the-mill friendly fixture, this would prove to be one of the most formative experiences of my career. The ACC worked on a 'winner stays on' basis, and the reigning champions – a Czechoslovakian Army team called Dukla Prague – had triumphed in the two previous years. Though this may conjure up images of ultra-fit bruisers, they proved to be one of the most tactically astute teams I'd ever faced.

The previous summer, I'd watched on television as the bulk of their team had finished runners-up to Brazil in the World Cup in Chile, with Czechoslovakia taking the lead before falling to a 3-1 defeat. With such an overlap in personnel between Dukla Prague and the national team, it came as little surprise that their attacking play was fuelled by the same purpose and guile that had momentarily caught out the Brazilians.

We succumbed to a 2-1 aggregate defeat over the course of our two matches against Dukla Prague but we considered our time in New York to be an overwhelming success. I top-scored, averaging more than a goal a game, and Bobby

Moore collected the Eisenhower Trophy, awarded to the Most Valuable Player in the tournament. More than goals and trophies, we came away better players for the challenge, learning from the teams we faced.

Two players in particular stood out for me, making an indelible impression. Unsurprisingly, both of these were Dukla Prague players. The first was the acclaimed star of the team and of Czech football in general: Josef Masopust. Crowned European Footballer of the Year for 1962, he gained widespread admiration for his dribbling throughout the World Cup and for the small matter of putting the Czechs ahead in the final. Due to the lack of exposure afforded to Dukla Prague, however, his reputation has faded considerably over time. This, I assure you, is unjust.

In those two games I saw enough of Masopust to rank him among the best playmakers I had ever come across, and more than 50 years on I feel that as strongly as ever. He could dribble with speed and control that utterly bewildered defenders and his pinpoint passing meant he was practically unstoppable at times. I'm not alone in thinking this, either. Many of his opponents were moved to publicly appreciate his abilities, not least Pelé. Speaking after the World Cup final that he had missed through injury, Pelé said: 'With those explosive dribbles, he had to be Brazilian.' High praise indeed.

The other player who caught my eye was Josef Jelínek, a forward and another member of the Czechoslovakian World Cup side. With Masopust pulling the strings for club and country, it was Jelínek's job to make sure they were untangled at all times. He stood out from the very start of our first match against them – the strangeness of his movement and positioning made it almost impossible not to take note. Unlike most forwards at the time, he was not solely focused on finding himself in goal-scoring positions, and his teammates reaped the rewards. This fair-haired forward ran tirelessly, dragging our defenders this way and that. It was relentless, unlike anything I'd seen before.

What's more, as our defenders tried to second-guess him, choosing to call his bluff, he soon found spaces opening for himself. This unselfish brand of running had yet to reach English shores, and as such it provided me with an important tactical edge when I returned.

Although he operated in the shadow of his teammate, Jelínek's approach was far more replicable. Masopust's technical ability simply could not be taught, but Jelínek's ingenuity and attitude certainly could. Either way, when these two Czechoslovakian schemers combined, the result was verging on mesmeric. So while it's Josef Masopust who makes the list at number 21, I cannot pass up the opportunity to give Jelínek an honourable mention. Two fine players whose reputation has suffered due only to the relative obscurity of their national league.

20. CAFU (Marcos Evangelista de Moraes)

If the 2014 World Cup in Brazil taught us anything, it's that the host nation is sorely lacking a defensive stalwart. The widely held view of Brazil is that they've always been a side consisting of ten attacking players. It would be eleven if the goalkeeper had his way. In truth they've only ever been able to enjoy success when they've had one or two solid and defensive-minded players in their back line. Yet the side hailed by many in Brazil as the greatest ever, the phenomenal 1982 team boasting Zico and Sócrates, lacked a defensive organiser and paid the price.

Thiago Silva was tipped by many to be the man to play this role in 2014 but after needlessly missing the 7-1 drubbing at the hands of Germany – he was suspended after blocking Colombia's keeper mid-dropkick – and by desperately hauling down Arjen Robben to concede a penalty in the opening minutes of the third place playoff, any illusions of dependability were emphatically destroyed. Though most Brazilians would never admit it, a team can't win trophies with attackers alone.

When Cafu made his World Cup debut in USA 1994, Brazil were a team in transition. Much to the displeasure of the fans, manager Carlos Alberto Parreira gave holding midfielder Dunga a prominent role in the team, even making him captain midway through the tournament. Though greatly effective, he represented the gritty, destructive side of the game that the fans simply refused to embrace and, despite being crowned World Champions, his time as captain is remembered as a low point in Brazil's football history.

Reliable doesn't have to mean boring, though, as right wingback Cafu proved in an international career spanning sixteen years and four World Cups. Managing to strike the right balance between defence and attack, he endeared himself to the Brazilian public from the very start. While Dunga faced derision from the terraces, Cafu enjoyed great adulation – for his was an approach to defending that the fans could enjoy. When he won the ball it was with the intention of attacking once more, whereas they felt Dunga simply slowed games down.

Like Carlos Alberto years before him, Cafu made the right flank his own. Dominating in defence and venturing forward at will, he was a formidable presence that few teams ever got

the better of. To add to this, Roberto Carlos arrived on the international scene shortly after Cafu, and the left back with the gigantic thighs and unstoppable shot provided a mirror image on the opposite wing. This symmetry formed the foundation of Brazilian success for years to come, enabling incisive counter-attacking play or complete dominance of possession depending on the game plan.

Cafu's two World Cup wins were standout moments in his career but he was equally successful at club level. A bugbear of many Brazilian supporters is the tendency of their better players to leave for Europe at the first opportunity instead of remaining loyal to their domestic leagues. Despite spending over half of his career in Italy, Cafu won favour firstly in a five-year stay at São Paulo (one of Brazil's biggest clubs), but also by showing little reluctance in returning to the country after a brief but successful spell with Zaragoza, spending a season at Juventude.

The high regard in which he is held by every club he played for is a hallmark of his professionalism, giving his all for his team and making it near-impossible to resent him when he chose to move on. This is true of Roma fans, who enjoyed five years of his service in which he claimed his first Serie A title – and they held no grudges when in 2003 he moved to AC Milan and really began to decorate his trophy cabinet.

Winning the UEFA Super Cup almost immediately, his first season ended with a further Serie A winner's medal, but the highlight of his Milan stay came in 2007 as he added a much-coveted Champions League winner's medal to his ever-growing collection. Though an unused substitute in the final and a veteran at 36 years of age, he had been deployed regularly by manager Carlo Ancelotti late on in games, using his experience to close out vital matches. After his years of service to the Italian giants, no one could argue that his medal wasn't richly deserved.

In a press conference, Sir Alex Ferguson once jokingly asked whether Cafu had two hearts, on account of his tireless running and unstinting stamina. An admirable quality in itself, when this commitment is coupled with a great defensive mind and a flair for attacking forays, the result is a manager's dream. As I'm sure was recognised by the majority of his managers, when it came to the right back slot Cafu was the complete package. It's not often I find myself waxing lyrical about a defender, but Cafu was that and so much more.

19. LUIS SUÁREZ

When I first drew up this list Luis Suárez was higher than nineteenth position. But when I first drew up this list Luis Suárez had not dug his teeth into Giorgio Chiellini's back and then tried to argue his way out of punishment. Admittedly, he had previously bitten two other players, but I believe in redemption and his performances and conduct throughout the 2013/14 season had done enough to convince me that he was a changed man. Evidently, I was wrong.

The shameful incident that overshadowed Uruguay's involvement in the 2014 World Cup gave me reason to reassess my definition of greatness. Obviously his misdemeanours do not make him any less capable of scoring great goals, apart from during his ever-lengthening suspensions, but they do make me less inclined to call him great.

In my opinion, the greatest footballers transcend the sport. They act as ambassadors for the game and understand their role in the world outside of football. This responsibility is no less vital than the duty to avoid needless suspensions so as not to handicap your teammates. You can accept the odd loss of control – we're all human, after all – but when your lapses of self-control result in months on the sidelines there really is no excuse. On too many occasions Luis Suárez has failed to maintain these standards and, in terms of this list at least, it leaves him needing to be a pretty special player to make up for that.

So enough about Suárez's shortcomings (far too much has already been said about them in recent months anyway), and let's instead focus on the positives, the aspects of his game that I had delighted in discussing before his latest moment of madness switched the focus.

As the goals were flying in throughout the 2013/14 season and Liverpool enjoyed their most exciting League campaign for years, I took the chance to discuss the Uruguayan with two Liverpool legends: Roger Hunt and Ian Callaghan. At the time, they were fortunate enough to see him play almost every week and so were able to speak with some authority about his strengths. They directed my attention towards one particular aspect of his game.

It's always difficult to get a complete appreciation without seeing them play live, as so much of a player's contribution is what they do off the ball and often out of the television camera's shot. For all the name-calling and the many accusations levelled against Luis Suárez throughout his career, you cannot claim that he is a greedy player. His tireless running is part of what makes him such an impressive teammate, but Roger and Ian were talking about more than mere harrying.

Playing in a Liverpool side that came to be lauded for the speed and unpredictability of its attacking play, Suárez was the man that most defences focused their efforts on stopping, given his unrivalled goal haul. Realising this, he had started to adopt a habit of making runs down blind alleys, away from the action, with the sole intention of opening up gaps in the defence for his teammates.

The sceptical among you will doubtless argue that this is simply attributing intelligence to what could well have been little more than poorly thought-out runs. This highlights the value of seeing games live. On numerous occasions when Suárez embarked on these selfless runs he visibly and animatedly gestured to the player in possession to not pass him the ball, pointing instead to a teammate in space. This is an admirable characteristic, a great display of camaraderie, but I was more impressed by the effectiveness with which he pulled it off.

The deep understanding of the game that is required to achieve this is indicative of a player who is operating at a level above that of the other players on the pitch, someone who is controlling the game. Add to this his more easily observable traits – his clinical finishing, fantastic balance, impeccable close control – and you are left with the man who, for long periods in that season, was the best player on the planet.

This side of Luis Suárez, a player who at his peak is able to score from just about anywhere on the pitch, is what makes him impossible to ignore when considering the greats of the game. After his assault on Chiellini, it was tempting to remove him from the list altogether, but the performances that convinced Barcelona to shell out more than £70 million for him meant that I couldn't overlook him.

I sincerely hope that over the course of the next few seasons, Suárez will focus on producing the sort of moments of brilliance that will live long in the memory and resolve his issues. There's no better place for him to do so than the Nou Camp, which is not to detract from the support he received during his time at Anfield, but playing alongside such supreme talents as Lionel Messi, Andrés Iniesta and Neymar will hopefully see him standing out from the illustrious crowd for reasons other than controversy.

18. DUNCAN EDWARDS

Duncan Edwards was admittedly a player I didn't see all that much of, and sadly this is true for most football fans. The lasting impression he made on Bobby Charlton, his fellow 'Busby Babe', and the stories Bobby has regaled me with over the years were enough for me to consider him as one of the greatest ever to play the game. In fact, everyone who was fortunate enough to see him play in his tragically brief career described him in the same awestruck manner.

Cementing his place in the first team at Manchester United before he had even reached his eighteenth birthday, he played predominantly on the left-hand side of defence but regularly burst forward to unleash devastating shots. With all the attributes to succeed in any position, it was not uncommon to see him deployed elsewhere on the pitch so as to subject the unprepared to his talents.

Between 1953 and 1958, the excitement surrounding Edwards was unavoidable. His manager and teammates spoke of him in the loftiest of terms. Matt Busby said, 'I rate Duncan Edwards the most complete footballer in Britain –

perhaps the world', while Bobby Charlton adds, 'I always felt I could compare well with any player, except Duncan. He was such a talent, I always felt inferior to him.'

Edwards was well on his way to establishing himself as one of the pre-eminent names in world football when on 6 February 1958 he boarded the ill-fated British European Airways flight 609 from Belgrade to Manchester. After stopping to refuel in Munich, two take-off attempts were aborted due to ominous noises coming from the engines amid heavy snowfall. When a third attempt was finally put into action, the plane failed to gain height and crashed into a fence surrounding the runway. The plane burst into flames with 38 passengers and crew on board.

Of the 22 lives claimed in the blaze, seven were Manchester United players, their average age just 24. Duncan Edwards was severely injured and, revealing his strength of will and fighting spirit, battled valiantly before losing his life more than two weeks later on 21 February. The news spread throughout the world of football and beyond, devastating his adoring supporters, not least Bobby Charlton. He has described it as the worst moment of his life, as a true friend and teammate was taken long before his time.

The man they came to call 'Man-boy' on account of his huge physical presence at such a young age showed so much promise in his short career. It is highly likely that, had he survived, he would have a World Cup winner's medal to his name – perhaps sooner than 1966, too – because he was showing all the signs of becoming a huge asset for England for years to come. His teammate, captain and another of those lost to the disaster, Roger Byrne, had also become a regular fixture in the England set-up with more than 30 caps. So too had Tommy Taylor, a prolific centre forward who scored over 100 times for Manchester United and who was

26 at the time of the crash. With these players in their prime, England could have been a real force in Chile in '62, where we lost out in the quarter-finals to eventual winners Brazil.

It's agonising to ponder what could have been, but even more painful to think of the lives that were lost. Duncan Edwards seemed to have the brightest of futures ahead of him. To consider him one of the greatest to ever play the game despite playing for only five years, long before he would have reached his prime, is admittedly a big claim to make – but I am not alone in thinking this. Although my selecting him is largely based on the potential he was tragically unable to fully realise, he had already shown so much promise in his short life, astounding great players like Bobby Charlton with his abilities. Had the cruellest of fates not intervened, then it is far from fanciful to think that he might have topped this list outright.

17. JOHN CHARLES

You could be forgiven for thinking that John Charles' career was in fact a less believable blueprint for that of Roy Race. The man who came to be known as Il Gigante Buono, The Gentle Giant, when he moved to Italy, enjoyed a career spanning four decades and three countries. He has taken on an almost mythical status since his playing days, particularly in Leeds and Turin where his name is uttered in the most reverent of tones.

Having joined Leeds United in late 1948, making the move from amateur football in his home town of Swansea, he began his career as a versatile defender playing in a number of positions across the back line. The world was still recovering from the Second World War and the military background of Leeds' manager, Major Frank Buckley, was very much a sign of the times.

By the time his first full season with the West Yorkshire club came to an end in the summer of 1950, Charles had turned eighteen and was called up for National Service. The Army made some concessions given his fledgling career, allowing him to return to Elland Road to play but insisting that he turn out for the Army team as well. His commitments saw him play a reduced role at Leeds, but his exposure to a range of sports in the Army only acted to improve him as a sportsman.

When his two years were up he had become a proficient basketball player and was strongly encouraged to pursue a career in boxing, having greatly impressed the boxing coaches in the forces. Thankfully for Leeds and football as a whole, he persevered with his first love.

Things had changed at Leeds during his partial absence, and he returned to find his role in the team much altered. They were struggling for goals and so Major Buckley decided to put Charles up front. It was a gamble, but given the Welshman's versatility and improved aerial ability, courtesy of his basketball training, it was worth a try. It turned out to be an inspired move.

In the 1952/53 season he scored 26 League goals, much to the delight of his fans and manager, but the best was yet to come. The following year he struck 42 times, averaging more than a goal a game, as it became clear that Leeds had a star in their ranks. His goals eventually secured promotion for Leeds in 1956, moving them up into the First Division for the first time in nine seasons. Once there, he didn't pause for breath, scoring 38 times in his first top-flight season.

Naturally, such goal-scoring ability can pass under the radar in the Second Division, but once in the First Division Leeds were powerless to hide him from potential suitors. In 1957 Juventus of Italy came calling. The Italian league was considered to be of a higher calibre than the English equivalent at the time and this was reflected by the payment on offer. Juventus offered £65,000 for Charles – who had scored 154 goals in his 316 games at Leeds – and he left with the best wishes of everyone at the club. He would return to Leeds later in his career for a brief half-season, and the club honoured Charles by naming a stand after him in 2004.

He immediately won favour with his new supporters, continuing in Italy as he had left off in England by scoring 28 times as the club were crowned champions of Italy. To put his impact into perspective, the two seasons prior to his arrival had seen Juventus finish joint ninth, although the signing of Charles' Argentinian strike partner Omar Sívori also played a part in this marked improvement.

His performances were enough to secure him the ultimate reward – a place in Wales' 1958 World Cup squad. He scored Wales' only goal in their opening group game as they drew 1-1 with Hungary before his side progressed to a glamorous quarter-final against Brazil. It was a day that would go down in history, but not for the reasons Charles might have hoped. Injury sidelined him for the match as another World Cup first-timer stole the show. I suppose there's no shame in being overshadowed by Pelé, even at the age of seventeen.

It was a close-fought battle requiring a bit of Pelé magic to make the difference and it was felt that, had Charles been fit, Wales could well have pushed Brazil all the way. Considering how much of a launch-pad that World Cup was for the great Brazilian, his Welsh counterpart could have enjoyed similar adulation had injury not interrupted his tournament. Alas, it wasn't to be, but Charles returned to Italy with his reputation further enhanced.

He continued to enjoy great success with the Turin side, claiming two more league titles and two Italian Cups before winding down with a meandering route to retirement – including the revisiting of his Leeds days and spells with AS Roma, Cardiff City, Hereford United and Merthyr Tydfil of Wales.

His love of the game was clear for all to see, and this saw him turn to management in his later days. It was also evident in the way he played the game. Over the course of his long career, he was never booked. Not once. Nor was he sent off. Standing at 6ft 2in and with a physique that made him an asset to the Army, he was often targeted with aggression, players feeling the need to try to tackle this Goliath head-on, but he wouldn't retaliate – hence the nickname of The Gentle Giant. There's just an inescapable romance surrounding John Charles. Voted by Juventus fans in 1998 as their greatest ever foreign player, and included in Leeds United's greatest XI (as a defender, no less!), he was truly loved by all those who saw him play. Roy Race, eat your heart out.

16. FERENC PUSKÁS

Without the use of footage or history books as proof, today you'd face a real challenge trying to convince most youngsters that Hungary were once the most feared outfit in world football. Given their current modest standing in the global game, this comes as little surprise, but I fear you'd face the same difficulties when trying to convince them that a man named Ferenc Puskás could do things with the ball that Gareth Bale could only dream of.

Football moves on, that's only natural, but we owe it to sides as influential as the Magnificent Magyars to make sure their legend lives on for decades to come. Between 1950 and 1956 they were rarely bettered. Hungary ruled the footballing world and during this six-year period achieved a quite startling record. Before defeat finally came in the final of the 1954 Swiss World Cup against West Germany (a match which was later dubbed 'The Miracle of Berne' due to the magnitude of the shock), Hungary had gone 49 games unbeaten, winning 42 and drawing seven. Their sheer dominance and the exciting attacking nature of their play only adds to the frustration that this great side was allowed to fade without so much as a major trophy to their name, although 'fade' is perhaps too soft a word for their demise.

Though Puskás is now better known for his achievements in Spain, when the Hungarian national side was at its peak every player in that team was still playing their club football in Hungary. However in 1956 as the Cold War escalated, unrest broke out across the nation culminating in the Hungarian Revolution. Though a number of players opted to stay, the majority put their career on hold to seek safety in foreign lands. It wasn't until two years later that Puskás finally began playing again, signing for Real Madrid. He was joined in Spain by his long-time strike partner Sándor Kocsis and flying winger Zoltán Czibor, although they would not get the chance to link up with Puskás on the pitch, instead signing for rivals Barcelona.

This influx of talent contributed to the supremacy of the Spanish leagues; meanwhile, the Hungarian league was left in tatters. It goes without saying that the destruction of Hungary's footballing heritage pales in comparison to some of the atrocities carried out during the Cold War, but were it not for the ongoing strife, teams such as MTK Hungária and Budapest Honvéd could well have become major forces in Europe.

One player who stayed behind and who was viewed by many to be on a par with Puskás was Nándor Hidegkuti. He had been instrumental in both 1953 and 1954 when Hungary had humiliated England, 6-3 and 7-1 respectively. Five years older than Puskás, he was in his mid-thirties at the time of the uprising so the idea of beginning a new overseas career held less promise. He retired two years later and Hungary's national team effectively went with him.

After leaving in 1956, Puskás never played another competitive game for a Hungarian side. He made such an impression on his new hosts that he eventually turned out for Spain's national side, even playing alongside his Argentinian-born Real Madrid teammate Alfredo Di Stéfano in a World Cup qualifier against Morocco in 1961. Although the pair only played a handful of games for the national side, their success at club level mirrored Puskás' form from his Hungary days.

His signing was initially derided by the locals; after all, he had spent more than a year out of the game. Naturally he had fallen slightly out of shape as a result and, with Madrid having just won La Liga and their second consecutive European Cup, many fans considered it an insult to the great Real Madrid side that such an unfit individual might be added to the squad. It didn't take him long to win over the supporters.

Legend has it that when Puskás first joined up with Los Merengues the club's director, Antonio Calderón, asked Di

Stéfano's opinion of their new acquisition. Di Stéfano was well known for demanding the same high standards of his teammates as those he maintained himself and he had a big say in what went on at the club, so the answer had the potential to impact heavily upon Puskás' career. Di Stéfano's response to Calderón was thus: 'He controls the ball with his left foot better than I can with my hand.'

With that much admired left foot, he proceeded to light up Real Madrid's attack for the next eight seasons, managing to do the unthinkable and provide a threat equal to that of Di Stéfano to form an unstoppable force. He scored 242 goals in 262 games, collecting five league titles and three European Cups along the way. All this despite not joining up with the Spaniards until he was 31 years of age. To put his goal-scoring feats into perspective, as of the summer of 2014 only Raúl, Di Stéfano and Carlos Santillana had ever scored more times for the club, though Cristiano Ronaldo looks set to join those select few. It should be noted that of these four names, only Ronaldo has a goals-to-game ratio capable of rivalling Puskás who scored on average a goal every 0.93 games.

Puskás' reputation for scoring beautiful goals resulted in the naming of a new award in his honour in 2009. The FIFA Puskás Award is given to the individual who scores the most visually impressive goal that year. When you consider all of the great goal scorers in the history of the game, it speaks volumes that his was the name chosen as the title for this award. It's pleasing to see that, after all these years, steps are being taken to preserve his legacy and pay homage to a product of the great era in Hungarian football.

15. DENIS LAW

Very few men make the switch from one half of Manchester to the other. Fewer still can consider both sides as their fans but for Denis Law that is very much the case. In more recent years Peter Schmeichel and Andy Cole made the switch in the twilight of their careers and did so without upsetting too many, but at the time these players made the move the two sides tended to be separated by ten league places and the chances of a meaningful head-to-head (beyond matters of civic pride) were slim.

This was very much Denis Law's thinking when he returned to Manchester City, the team that had given him his first taste of top-flight football, following a decade of unstinting success at their city rivals United. He departed Old Trafford having played a central role in the club's rebuilding process in the wake of the Munich air disaster. With a persistent knee injury restricting appearances in his final season with the Reds, a campaign which saw him score only once in the league, Law was allowed to leave on a free transfer in 1973.

Winning an FA Cup, two First Division titles and a European Cup during his stay at Old Trafford, he had good reason to be confident that his legacy could survive one last season at the club that had given him his big break. Of course it did, as his statue outside Old Trafford shows, but one of the cruellest twists of fate in football history challenged even his most loyal of fans from the red half of the city to refrain from cursing his name.

With a rehabilitated knee, he managed to rack up 30 appearances for City over the course of the 1973/74 season. Their final game of the season, one that had looked like the perfect swansong for Law when the fixtures were announced, pitted them against a United side languishing in the relegation zone. What could have been a dream sign-off became a nightmare fixture, laced with the possibility of inflicting great pain on his former team and, by extension, himself.

Almost inevitably, with the game goalless after 80 minutes, a rampaging City attack involving Mike Summerbee, Franny Lee and Colin Bell resulted in a pass to an unmarked Law, six yards out with his back to goal. Instinctively he swept the ball behind him with an effortless back heel, beating a flat-footed Alex Stepney. Denis froze before the Old Trafford crowd. As his teammates mobbed him in jubilation he grimaced, half raising a hand as if to apologise to his former employers. The famous celebration, the lofted arm with the sleeve gripped tightly in hand, was noticeably absent. The haunted look on his face was clear for all to see and his manager relieved him of his duties, substituting him almost immediately upon request.

Though it later transpired that results elsewhere had rendered Law's strike meaningless, at least in terms of the relegation battle, it was the reluctant seal on Manchester United's relegation. He later summed up the events of the day, saying: 'After nineteen years of trying my hardest to score goals, here was one that I almost wished hadn't actually gone in.' The evident anguish the goal caused him drew sympathy from the home fans and respect from the wider footballing community. An unfortunate footnote to his career, it ensured that both the blue and the red half of Manchester would forever look upon him with great fondness.

This may well be the moment most City fans and neutrals remember him for, but United fans have over 400 games' worth of moments to choose from, including 237 goals.

Teaming up with George Best and Bobby Charlton to form what became known as the 'Holy Trinity', the man they called 'The King' was an ever-reliable presence in one of the most potent attacks in world football.

That day in April '74 wasn't the only time he lined up against some of his fellow stars from that great Manchester United side of the 1960s. With a side consisting of so many British internationals, games against his clubmates were inescapable, especially in the era of Home Internationals. Nobby Stiles tells a tale of England versus Scotland games when the two found themselves on opposing sides. When Nobby walked over to Denis, a proud Scotsman, he was simply ignored. Despite making attempts to engage him in light-hearted conversation, Denis's message was clear and blunt – 'Get lost!' Personally, this only makes me admire him more; his passion and commitment to his team's cause was such that even one of his closest friends was the enemy for those 90 minutes. The spirit of a true winner.

The moments I best remember him for came before his Manchester days and away from the international scene, when he was still making a name for himself at Huddersfield Town in Division Two. I was a junior at West Ham at the time, and we drew Huddersfield in the FA Cup in January 1960. Having drawn the initial tie away at their old Leeds Road stadium, we met for the replay a few days later at Upton Park. I was watching on from the stands as the two teams tried to get to grips with the icy conditions. As the nineteen other outfield players slipped and stumbled, Denis Law moved about the pitch with such poise and balance, almost as though he was wearing ice skates instead of football boots.

He pulled the strings as Huddersfield beat us 5-1, a performance that contributed to his eventual departure

from the club a couple of months later to join Manchester City for a British record transfer fee of £55,000. All those in attendance were acutely aware that they were witnessing a special talent and so it was little surprise to me that he went on to achieve such great things. His performance that day revealed his greatest trait, his split-second reactions. I've yet to see a player who could react as quickly and purposefully as Denis could, an ability that had the potential to change games in an instant.

A great player, a great man and a professional to the very end, Denis Law is someone who I will always feel privileged to have seen play.

14. GERD MÜLLER

Without wanting to lean too heavily on stereotypes, it really can be a job to avoid terms like 'efficiency' and 'consistency' when describing the goal scorers Germany has produced over the years and seemingly continues to turn out.

The latest off the production line is Bayern Munich's Thomas Müller, a Golden Boot winner in his first World Cup and only narrowly missing out on the award in his second. When he scored his tenth World Cup finals goal in Germany's historic 7-1 demolition of host Brazil in July 2014, he became the fifth German ever to reach double figures. To put this into perspective, other than Brazil, no other nation has seen more than one player reach this landmark.

Pundits and commentators have built up an arsenal of descriptions to politely say that, despite his goals, Thomas

Müller doesn't seem to be particularly great. Excepting his ability to force the ball over the line it really is difficult to identify an area of his game where he excels. He's good at lots of things, of course he is, but he just seems to be a solid seven or eight out of ten in every aspect apart from scoring. His stamina is arguably the exception, but that's not going to get anyone off their seat. Nobody's actually even certain what position he plays in – somewhere in midfield is the closest we've come to categorising him. Yet while he may not be great, there are precious few who are better. To be so ruthless in front of goal despite never really standing out has enabled him to rack up an impressive goals tally (roughly one every three games).

He had a chance to learn from the master, Miroslav Klose, who in 2014 forced his way to the top of the all-time World Cup goal scorers' list, having netted in four consecutive tournaments, a quite remarkable achievement. His sixteenth World Cup finals goal moved him one ahead of Brazil's Ronaldo. The pair were both phenomenal goal scorers, but their strikes could not have been more different. While Ronaldo often scored flamboyant, audacious efforts, Klose scored every single one of his from between the penalty spot and the goal. Right place, right time, cool finish.

Though many won't appreciate the skill this takes, it really is an art form. To time your runs, to lose your man, you have to be constantly thinking and assessing your position. It requires great awareness and, even though these strikes are usually fairly simple, it also requires a calm head. Before Klose, before Ronaldo and long before Thomas Müller there was someone who did this better than anyone. Gerd Müller, the man whose World Cup goals record stood for more than three-and-a-half decades. The most impressive thing was that Müller only needed two tournaments to rack up his

fourteen goals. Ten of them came in Mexico in 1970 and this remains the third biggest single-tournament total to date, only falling short of Just Fontaine's thirteen in Sweden in 1958 and Hungarian Sándor Kocsis's eleven in Switzerland four years earlier.

It becomes increasingly dull to dig any deeper than that when analysing Müller's World Cup record but the temptation to do so is strong, as Gerd Müller's greatness cannot be summed up by describing a single goal in a lovingly curated highlights reel. His greatness lies in his goal-scoring records. In 62 games for West Germany he scored 68 times but still he was a pundit's nightmare. Short of identifying the defender who should have picked him up, the vast majority of his goals defied analysis. He made the beautiful game look simple.

Obviously other nations have had their poachers too. Italy's Paolo Rossi, Croatia's Davor Šuker and even our very own Gary Lineker epitomised this diligent role, but each of them had far more of a tendency to wander than Müller ever did. Even Filippo Inzaghi, a player who spent the bulk of his career lurking in the six-yard box, couldn't get close to Gerd Müller's strike rate.

The great West German marksman excelled at something that is ridiculed in the playgrounds and on the playing fields of Britain, dismissed as the shameful act of 'goal hanging'. Tap-ins and close range headers just don't bring the same glory as a strike from range or a curled effort from outside the box. They're seen as lazy and not in the spirit of the game. But in Germany these strikes are recognised as a route to ultimate glory. Gerd Müller perfected an approach to goal scoring that looks from afar like absolute child's play, but if it's so simple then how come we're not all doing it?

13. JIMMY GREAVES

On 9 June 2009, World Cup winners' medals were awarded to those members of the 1966 squad who were not included in the eleven that contested the final. More than four decades overdue, FIFA finally acknowledged their mistake in not awarding medals to the squad as a whole and bestowed the same retrospective honour upon all World Cup-winning squad players from 1930 up to 1974.

It served as a timely reminder of some of the forgotten greats from that era. Many of the names are still the topic of regular discussion among fans of their former clubs, such as Norman Hunter, Peter Bonetti and Ian Callaghan. The same is undoubtedly true of Jimmy Greaves, but it has become increasingly apparent to me that his career has slipped from the collective consciousness of football fans in recent years.

In much the same way that my career was defined by my performance in the World Cup final, Jimmy's seems to have been remembered for his injury in the final group game and his subsequent omission. This despite being the third top scorer in England's history and with a goals-per-game ratio far superior to those ahead of him.

The severity of the problem was brought home to me recently when talking to the nephew of one of my neighbours, a nineteen-year-old lad called Luke. Naturally we got to talking about football and as Jimmy's name entered the conversation I started to notice a blank look on his face. 'You do know who Jimmy Greaves is, don't you?' I asked him. Still, that blank look and a shake of the head. Oh boy. So I sat him down and started to reel off Jimmy's record. He had little say in the matter.

Beginning with Chelsea at sixteen years of age; 169 games, 132 goals; the youngest player to score 100 goals in English league football at twenty years and 290 days old. Luke started to pay attention. Jimmy scored a debut goal for every team he played for including three in his first game at Tottenham, a club for which he remains the all-time leading league goal scorer with 220 goals. The first player to top the First Division goal-scoring charts three years running and finally – 44 goals in 57 games for England. And all this in an era when strikers were regularly barged and kicked off the ball within the laws of the game. Suffice it to say I'd got the message across to young Luke by this point, but that didn't stop me quizzing him on Jimmy's record for the rest of the evening.

I still keep in regular contact with Jimmy and we're often invited to speak at events together, especially ones relating to the England team. One such event came in early 2014 during the World Cup tour, as the successor to the Jules Rimet trophy was taken to each and every FIFA delegation. Setting off in September 2013, the trophy departed Brazil for Tahiti before moving on to Fiji, Vanatu, Costa Rica and so on until finally in mid-March 2014 it touched down in England. Wembley Stadium was naturally chosen as a stop-off point and so Jimmy and I, along with Gordon Banks, were invited along to partake in a small breakfast panel, to be interviewed by Jim Rosenthal.

Now as many will know from his days as one half of Saint and Greavsie, Jimmy enjoys a chat and on that day he was on particularly good form. Prior to the event we were asked by FATV, the Football Association's online video service, to answer four or five quick questions on camera and naturally we agreed. Sitting in the stands overlooking the pitch, all was going well until they reached the fourth question, which they put to me first.

'What's the most important piece of advice you've received from a manager at half-time during an England game?' they asked. Not technically at half-time, but a hugely important team talk nonetheless, my answer was Sir Alf's message to us before extra time in the final, a game that we'd been leading until the 89th minute. Everyone gathered on the touchline as was commonplace and a few of the lads were sitting on the floor, resting. Sir Alf took one look at them and said, 'Get up, don't let the Germans see that you're tired,' not willing to give an inch in the psychological battle. Then he left us with one line which we all remember to this day: 'You've beaten them once, go and beat them again.' Simple but effective, this was exactly the pick-me-up we needed to get our heads right for an extra half-hour.

They then asked Banksy for his answer and he obliged as earnestly as I had, though I forget his exact answer. Next, they moved on to Jimmy. With the interviewer looking on intently, Jimmy began: 'I'll never forget, in the early days of my career when England played Scotland in a game at Wembley, Sir Alf Ramsey came in at half-time and said to me, "Put your fag out!"'

Bear in mind this was on FATV, going out to thousands of impressionable kids, so an air of professionalism would have been welcomed. It was about to get worse. He continued to speak with bemused faces staring back at him. 'Blow me, no sooner had Sir Alf told me to put mine out than he nips round the corner to have one himself!' Unsurprisingly, they wound up the interview shortly after.

Later that morning we were sitting in a small anteroom in Wembley, having tea and sandwiches with Jim Rosenthal before the show. Five representatives from FIFA then entered the room, one of whom was wearing white gloves and holding a small briefcase-like capsule containing the

World Cup. The white gloves are standard practice when holding any valuable memorabilia, but after a few minutes' conversation with these guys it emerged that, in the case of the World Cup, former winners are the only individuals excused from wearing the gloves when holding it. Quick as a flash, Jimmy pipes up and says, 'This poses a very interesting question – if the World Cup gets nicked, there's only our f**king finger prints on the thing!' By this time I was in tears. Thankfully, the panel show proceeded in a rather more courteous manner and we managed to leave Wembley without lifetime bans, but that's Jimmy for you – impossible to predict on or off the pitch.

I should stress that my fondness for Jimmy and my admiration of his ability has a lot to do with him being one of my generation. I can remember as a kid when being told about the players from days gone by, they just didn't resonate in the same way that my boyhood heroes did. I understand that. It's a shame but that's life. Yet a healthy respect is important, the sort of respect players of my generation have for Sir Stanley Matthews and Sir Tom Finney. It's always good to know your history and Jimmy is a big, big part of the history of English football.

12. FRANZ BECKENBAUER

Franz Beckenbauer. Der Kaiser. One of the most distinguished names in world football, few have ever achieved as much in the game. Having won the World Cup both as player and manager, so too the Bundesliga (five times as a player, once as manager), three European Cups as a player and countless individual awards, his record speaks for itself. His story is far more than just trophies, though, and one that crossed over with mine on so many occasions.

When players look back on their careers, they tend to be reminded of four key occasions: their first, last, best and worst games. All four of mine came against West Germany, shared between three matches. Each and every time, Franz Beckenbauer was present.

I made my international debut at Wembley in February 1966 in a friendly which, unbeknown to us, would turn out to be a dry run of the World Cup final later that year. A rare goal from Nobby Stiles, who oddly happened to be wearing the number 9 shirt, ensured my first cap was marked with a victory. Still only twenty years of age, Beckenbauer was rather subdued in that fixture. I have to admit that even after that game I knew very little of the man.

When we next met five months later, however, we had studied him more than any other player in the World Cup. During the tournament we had the games piped through to our base on a big screen. We'd all gather around to watch and see what we could work out about our potential opponents. When we sat down to watch West Germany vs. Switzerland, a group stage match held at Sheffield Wednesday's Hillsborough stadium, Sir Alf Ramsey spotted the danger-man almost immediately.

Sauntering through the Swiss defence with ease, Beckenbauer scored twice, showing off his full range of attacking and defensive qualities in a commanding 5-0 win. It was an explosive start to the tournament for the young German and he seemed to grow as a player with each game. By the time the final came around our first objective was to keep him quiet. As we later found out, their manager

Helmut Schön was making similar provisions for Bobby Charlton. Thankfully for us, the two managers reached the same decision as each gave their star man the task of marking the other.

With these two players effectively nullified, the game essentially became ten vs. ten. This heightened the importance of the West Ham connection as Martin, Bobby and I were in the habit of linking up and were well equipped to cope with having the central cog removed from our machinery. And so my greatest day in football came to pass. A moment we savoured all the more because of the quality of opponent we had to overcome. Though there were plenty more highpoints to come in my career, in terms of my head-to-heads with Beckenbauer it was all downhill thereafter.

Although this was in some part due to the ageing of key members of our squad and also the untimely loss of Gordon Banks to sickness ahead of our defeat in the Mexico World Cup of 1970, Beckenbauer's progress as a player meant that his will was far more forcefully imposed in our meetings after '66. In my final game as an England international, the first leg of a European Championship qualifier, we saw Beckenbauer at his unstoppable best. Wembley Stadium was once again the setting, but the match was unlike any that I'd been involved in between the two nations, as we lost 3-1. Der Kaiser later remarked, 'I have never shared in a finer West German performance,' and I can believe it. It was the only time we took to a pitch to face them and simply couldn't compete.

It had always been hard to pin down Beckenbauer's position. He had started his international career operating predominantly as a central midfielder, but by '72 he had dropped far deeper. It made little sense to most of us watching on – why move your best player further away from the goal? It was in complete contrast to what we'd come to expect and seemed like a waste of his abilities. In practice, the effects were devastating. He created a whole new position for himself and delighted in making rampaging runs with the ball from the heart of his defence into the heart of the opposition's.

Football like any sport follows trends, especially in terms of training and tactics. When Beckenbauer began to forge his innovative role at the centre of the West German team it seemed inevitable that a whole host of Beckenbauer Mk IIs would spring up in teams across the globe, but the fact of the matter was that most teams didn't have a player capable of doing what he did. The role was embraced in a more defensive capacity by the Italians who liked to keep their defences bolted shut and sweepers such as Baresi (whom I've already admired in this book) would capitalise when attacks broke down, marshalling the ball away from danger and starting attacks.

Beckenbauer didn't simply marshal, though, and he was never content merely starting attacks. The years he spent as a midfielder meant that he was no less comfortable advancing beyond the halfway line than he was on the edge of his own box. He collected the ball, he pushed forward and he orchestrated attacks. He was the spine of the team, fulfilling the jobs that normally you'd expect to be spread between two or three players.

Though both are often described as liberos, Baresi and Beckenbauer's interpretation of the position differed hugely. In addition to the defensive positioning and attacking vision that are required to be a successful Baresi-esque sweeper, the Beckenbauer version needs so much more. To demonstrate close control while sprinting forth from defence and then have the requisite stamina to get back and snuff out consequent counter-attacks was beyond most players. His role was inimitable because he was inimitable.

If his playing career wasn't enough to drive you mad with jealousy, his ability to replicate his leadership skills in a managerial capacity should probably just about do it. There may have been a time when a nickname like Der Kaiser, or The Emperor, might have seemed grandiose but by the time he retired he had done everything imaginable to justify it.

11. GEORGE BEST

The legend of George Best has been told more times than most over the years. The boy from Belfast's Cregagh estate who would go on to be football's answer to The Beatles, he was the first footballing superstar as we know them today; as common a presence on the front page of newspapers as he was on the back. Unlike many of the players who now fill the tabloid press, Best had the footballing ability to justify his widespread fame.

As is now fairly common knowledge, he was in danger of not even making it as a footballer after a number of Irish teams considered him too small and lightweight to ever cut it against senior pros. The assumption nowadays is that he was able to overcome this thanks to his nimble footwork and agile body, but that was only part of the story.

The same slightness of body that was picked up on by Irish scouts and coaches was doubtless targeted by each and every team he came up against in his youth. By the time he came to sign pro forms with Manchester United in 1963 he had acquired a catalogue of coping techniques and I know from a number of my former teammates who were given the unenviable task of marking him that he delighted in putting them into practice. With razor-sharp elbows and feet that would stumble oh-so-carelessly upon toes at corners and in battles for space, Best knew how to level the playing field.

Though this may sound like the dirty underbelly of the beautiful game, it was simply a facet of a more physical era and was no worse than the treatment he received. More importantly, it won him the space and respect he needed to show off his true talents. This mindset was vital to succeed at the very top and, as is still the case today, if you could come out on top in the mental sparring then the rest of the task was made far easier. I too had to learn ways of coping with the more physical defenders, riding challenges when needed while convincing them that I could enter into a battle if it came to it. Had I not, then it's unlikely I would have made it through a game, season or career.

Having proven himself as a worthy opponent in his tussles for possession, when the ball fell at George's feet there were few who could match him. He once remarked that when watching clips of himself playing football, 'I always feel like I'm watching somebody else because it was totally off the cuff and that's the way I'd always been.' This was clear to see when watching him play. He could weave through crowds of players with the ball at his feet while maintaining better balance than many of those standing in his path. He didn't need to plan his route to goal. Appearing to change direction four or five times within the space of a few yards, he would often just sway his hips this way and that while letting the ball run on its natural course, toying with the opposition. As in his tussles with defenders, he'd often beaten his opponents before the move had begun, the mere

insinuation of a touch enough to send them stumbling and staggering out of his path.

This was what I loved most about watching George Best, about watching any great footballer for that matter. He was an entertainer above all else and was always worth paying to see. There were times when his superiority and his ability to embarrass defenders was so great that they simply refused to play. He once said: 'If I was playing against a player who was giving me a particularly hard time, I'd stand on the ball and tell him to come and get it off me. I loved it, it was pure theatre. I did it on purpose because I knew it got the crowd excited.'

His career is perhaps best remembered for his perform-ances against Benfica. In the 1966 European Cup quarter-final he played the starring role in Manchester United's 5-1 victory in Lisbon, becoming the first foreign side to taste victory at Estádio de Luz. They were knocked out in the next round by Partizan Belgrade but two years later Best was again central to the action as they went all the way. He scored the goal that broke the hearts and resolve of the Lisbon giants. Striking two minutes into extra time in the final of 1968, his goal set them on their way towards a historic 4-1 victory, poignantly clinching the trophy ten years on from the tragedy of the Munich air disaster. The win was hailed as the final brick in the rebuilding project.

In terms of prestige, these matches were the closest thing we have to seeing George Best tested at the highest level. With the standard of Northern Irish football lagging far behind his exemplary standards, he was never afforded the chance to compete in a World Cup but I have little doubt that he would have succeeded. In fact he and Alfredo Di Stéfano are probably the only two players that I can say with near certainty would have succeeded on the world stage. Having seen him almost singlehandedly tear apart that Benfica side which contained the bulk of the 1966 third-placed Portugal team, the team he had destroyed were an international opponent in all but name.

The off-field problems that saw his career peter out in his late twenties and ultimately cut short his life are still a cause for great sadness. It's always difficult to think that someone, especially someone as gifted as he, wasted some of their talent but Best packed more than enough into his time with Manchester United to be considered a great of the game. The fact that he is so highly revered despite never competing in a World Cup just goes to show how special a talent he really was. There is a saying in Belfast that goes, 'Maradona good, Pelé better, George Best.' While I don't agree with the ranking, on ability alone there really wasn't much in it.

10. BOBBY MOORE

Bobby Moore was, and remains to this day, my hero. He was the most dedicated professional I ever had the pleasure of playing alongside. And it really was a pleasure, every time we stepped out on to the field together, be it the training pitches at Chadwell Heath or Wembley Stadium for a World Cup final. He was the ultimate teammate; the ultimate centre half.

Having spent so much time together throughout our careers I'm not short of great memories of Mooro, but neither is anyone else who met him. He had such a likeable personality and was such a memorable man that everybody seems to have a nice tale to tell about him.

One story that I'm sure a lot of his former England teammates would tell you centres on his first World Cup with the side. Having snuck into the '62 World Cup squad at the last moment, a late replacement due to an injury in the camp, you might have expected him to just be thankful for his place, but Bobby wasn't the shy, retiring type. He quickly became one of the most active and noticeable players in the side, and much to his credit too.

Whereas most 21-year-olds would defer to their more senior counterparts, Mooro felt he was the best man to be taking free kicks and corners – so he did. These were normally decided on seniority and often subject to the older lads calling rank, so the potential for disharmony was palpable when this youngster took set-pieces into his own hands. Thankfully for Bobby, and as a result England, the senior pros could see all too clearly the making of a future captain in the bold youngster and so he got his way.

Bobby's greatest natural abilities were almost all to do with his mind and brain, self-confidence evidently being one example. His ability to read the game was phenomenal and both his timing in the tackle and his composure under pressure were exceptional. It was as though he saw the game at a different speed to everyone else. This gave him a fantastic base to build upon – but the ability to read the game is one thing, knowing how best to affect it requires practice and experience. It was Bobby's dedication to the latter that transformed him from a good player into a great one.

He joined West Ham shortly before I did (1956 and 1959 respectively) and when we first played together he was fairly green and certainly wasn't one of the outstanding players at the club. In fact, in his younger years he didn't even look athletic – schoolboy photos of him reveal a chubby little kid – but his drive to succeed ensured that every last drop of talent was squeezed out over the course of his career.

This was never more evident than when lunchtime arrived during pre-season sessions. With the 50 or so senior professionals joined by all of the youth team players, they used to get quite competitive – the old guard keen to set the bar high for the next generation. It became routine that, before breaking for lunch, every player would lie on their back and raise their feet off the ground. This is a basic exercise, one that tests core strength. A competitive element was introduced, with a prize on offer to whoever was the last player to let their feet drop. The prize was never anything special, usually just some orange segments, but the chance to win saw that Bobby was always the last man to touch his heels to the ground. Even in training he had to win – the sort of attitude that managers dream of seeing in their players.

He worked so hard on every single detail that it became almost inevitable he would achieve greatness. It extended beyond just his training – he endeared himself to journalists and paparazzi as well. In the same way in which every training drill had to be completed to the very best of his ability, he couldn't stand it if his kit wasn't absolutely perfect. He'd mill around the changing room before kick-off in full kit except for his shorts. He didn't want to crease them, so he left it until the very last moment to put them on.

It didn't end once he left the football ground, either, and it was picked up on by all who met him. One evening, back in our playing days, we were in a bar with former Manchester City striker Mike Summerbee. Bobby had been whisked away and engaged in conversation while Mike and I chatted on the other side of the room. Mike had been looking at Bobby almost open-mouthed for quite a while when he nodded over at him and said to me: 'Look at Mooro, he's the only player I know who irons his money!'

Fast forward 40-odd years, by which time Mike had deservedly been appointed as an ambassador for Manchester City. He and I found ourselves together in the boardroom at West Ham. Not remembering this conversation of four decades earlier, the subject of Bobby Moore came up once again. At this point it became clear just how big an impression he'd left on Mike, who offered up another of his colourful descriptions to me. 'You know, Geoff, Mooro was the only player I know who could have a bath and come out dry.'

I remember these stories with the broadest of smiles because it says all you really need to know about the man. The respect in which he is held by his former teammates, opposition and former pros is unrivalled. His tackle on Jairzinho in 1970, the image of us lofting him up in Wembley in '66, these stellar moments are recognised worldwide but you could see excellence in absolutely everything he did.

His obsession with perfection looked exhausting at times, at least from the outside. He always seemed to be in competition with someone or something, usually himself. His mind was fixated on how he could improve upon his current situation, be it his own ability or his team's position within a match. Whereas many players felt the pressure of big games, the challenge only seemed to improve Bobby's game. It rubbed off on his teammates too, because when Bobby was in the mood he didn't even need to ask for the ball. If anyone looked unsure on the ball he'd be there, helping them out before they even had a chance to flash him a nervous glance.

Former Chelsea manager Dave Sexton once said of him, 'Bobby Moore was an occasion player' – which doesn't initially sound altogether like a compliment. What Dave meant was that the big games spurred him on, as opposed to him only bothering when glory was at stake, and this was something I can say I noticed in him too. He'd have good games against weaker sides, often he'd be absolutely fantastic, but it was only when he was pitted against the best that you started to realise just how good a player he was. If the opposing forwards upped their game, so too would Bobby.

This is partly why it's harder to judge the greatness of defenders; attackers can shine against almost any opposition, be it through goals or flair play, but a defender only really gets credit when they stop the very best. When Bobby shone, though, it was impossible to miss it. That's why there's a statue of him outside Wembley. That's why West Ham have a stand named after him. It's why he was a World Cup-winning captain at the age of 25 and it's why it meant so much to me when, after a game against Sunderland in which I'd scored and assisted, he walked over to me and said, 'You're f**king brilliant and you know it.' It wasn't particularly poetic, but few words have ever meant more to me.

9. EUSÉBIO (Eusébio da Silva Ferreira)

Eusébio da Silva Ferreira. The name alone is enough to strike fear into defenders of a certain age and send the rest of us, both supporters and simply those of us with a penchant for playing higher up the pitch, into dreamy recollections of his attacking master classes.

Funnily enough, one of the most prominent memories I have of Eusébio is not one of him bursting through a defence or lashing a shot beyond a goalkeeper. It's not even one of him tackling back. Instead it's an almost comical clip of him doing battle with Nobby Stiles, or rather Nobby waging war on him. I can't recall whether the game in question was the 1968 European Cup Final between Man United and Benfica or the semi-final between us and Portugal in 1966, but it was reminiscent of countless tussles over the course of both fixtures.

The ball had been cleared out for a throw-in and, with Eusébio their greatest threat, the guy taking it was keen to get it back at the star man's feet and so proceeded to throw the ball to him. Before he could even think about controlling it, Nobby had clattered him – bam! – clearing it for another throw. Unfortunately for Eusébio, the taker hadn't learned his lesson, so once again he threw the ball in his direction. Nobby needed no invitation, again flying through the back of him and clearing the ball out of play. Watching this again years later, I was already in fits of laughter at his less than subtle approach to nullifying Eusébio, but what topped it all off was the sight of Nobby turning to the ref and gesturing that he was diving.

That was a snapshot from a different era. Had that game been played today, then Nobby would have doubtless received his marching orders, but more noteworthy was Eusébio's reaction. Now, the man was an absolute powerhouse and it would have taken a colossal effort from Nobby to cause any real damage, so after each robust challenge he simply clambered to his feet and dusted himself down. He didn't roll around or pretend to be injured. He just got up.

My fondness for Eusébio is encapsulated as much in this incident as it is in any one of his 733 career goals, which he rather astoundingly managed to score in just 745 appearances. His will to win was unshakeable and he played like a warrior at all times to achieve his aims. Even in the 1960s, one of the most physical periods in football history, his resilience and power stood out.

Make no mistake, our World Cup-winning side was tough.

We had the ability to add to this, but we knew how to handle ourselves against even the fiercest of opponents. It was rare that we came up against a side who could match us physically, but Eusébio was one of the few who were up to the challenge. His famous nickname, the Black Panther, was the perfect description. He stalked opponents with poise and grace, but had the ferocious power to leave them stricken at will. You daren't anger him either, as North Korea discovered to their cost in '66.

Unlike Portugal's 7-0 rout in South Africa in 2010 (a game which was overshadowed by stories of misreporting of the tournament in North Korea), when the two sides met in 1966 the East Asian side represented a far sterner task. More than 50,000 people packed into Everton's Goodison Park for the quarter-final, many of whom had turned up primarily to see Eusébio shine, but after 25 minutes it looked as though Portugal were not just going to lose, but be utterly humiliated in the process.

The North Koreans, having struck in the very first minute, found themselves 3-0 up and cruising; but before the stopwatch had reached the half-hour mark, Eusébio had set to work on one of the most unstoppable virtuoso performances in World Cup history.

We've all seen examples of games where the commentators chide the underdogs for having the audacity to score first, retrospectively claiming that 'their big mistake was to anger the opposition'. Brazil vs. Scotland in Spain '82 springs to mind, when David Narey opened the scoring spectacularly before a rampaging Brazil responded with four goals from four separate players. In North Korea's case, they knew the one man they had to stop but were powerless to resist.

Eusébio's first goal was set up by his clubmate, António Simões, a long threaded through ball which he coolly

swept home. The second was a powerfully struck penalty two minutes before half-time, and a further strike from open play levelled the scores ten minutes after the break. Portugal's attacking play was relentless and every time the ball fell to Eusébio the North Koreans looked panicked. This was highlighted best of all by his fourth goal, giving Portugal the lead for the first time in the match.

Running half the length of the pitch with the ball inexplicably fixed to his toe, he first held off the challenge of the midfielder who began to clip at his heels as they neared the penalty area. Eusébio then brushed past the full-back, slipping the ball between his static legs before slipping into the box. An air of inevitability swept through the stadium as North Korea's tormentor bore down on goal. This time they weren't prepared to let him get his shot away. First the nutmegged defender took a swipe at his heels, knocking him off balance, then the centre back came clattering across, completely ignoring the ball, to send him crashing to the ground. It was like watching young boys trying to tackle their dad in the park. Eusébio was superior in every aspect.

As if there were any doubt, Eusébio dispatched the penalty before another of his Benfica teammates, José Augusto, scored a header late on to wrap up proceedings. It was a majestic performance from a man at the top of his game and was rewarded by a semi-final against us at Wembley Stadium. Although we ended up as victors on the night, a consolation penalty from Eusébio seemed fitting, given his exploits in the previous games.

Portugal were a very good side, built around a strong foundation of Benfica players. Simões and Augusto formed part of this as I've already mentioned, along with captain Mário Coluna and centre forward José Torres. These players were vital to Eusébio's success, as Bobby Moore and Martin

Peters were to mine. The strong understanding you get from training and matches at club level can prove invaluable on the international stage. They provided the support Eusébio needed to shine and be recognised as one of the greatest of all time.

It was also important that Eusébio enjoyed relative success with both Portugal and Benfica during his career, at least in terms of establishing a lasting legacy. Benfica reached five European Cup finals throughout the 1960s, were crowned champions in 1961 and 1962, and were viewed as one of the world's biggest clubs as a result. Portugal, conversely, had never reached a World Cup until 1966 – they wouldn't reach another until 1986 – and so his role in leading them to a third place finish was arguably on a par with anything he achieved at club level. As a team they were treading new ground, and over the course of four weeks they wrote their names and their nation into the history books.

Eusébio took the chance that was never afforded to players like Alfredo Di Stéfano or George Best and made the most of it. For his achievements at club level alone, I would undoubtedly have included him among my 50, but the chance to see him shine in 1966 removed the most frustrating of all doubts – could he have cut it on the biggest stage?

8. ZINEDINE ZIDANE

In December 2013 I flew out to Bahia in Brazil to take part in the draw for the groups for the 2014 World Cup. I was joined by Alcides Ghiggia (a winner with Uruguay in 1950), Mario

Kempes (Argentina – 1978), Lothar Matthäus (West Germany – 1990), Cafu (Brazil – 1994, 2002), Zinedine Zidane (France – 1998), Fabio Cannavaro (Italy – 2006), and Fernando Hierro who appeared on behalf of Spain, the reigning World Champions at the time. Seven supremely talented men, it was an honour for me to be selected alongside them. On the day of the draw a van was sent to our hotel to collect us. I sat up front alongside Alcides Ghiggia – we knew our place as the senior members of the party – and the rest clambered in behind.

Immediately I was taken back to my playing days when, surrounded by unruly teammates, mischief hung in the air along with the scent of Fiery Jack and dubbin. Faced with lots of long, cramped journeys, we became quite inventive at finding ways to liven up these trips. One of the old favourites was to wait until the driver was navigating a narrow tunnel or reversing through a crowded car park, at which point someone (usually sitting towards the back) would bang on the inside of the van to make the poor bloke think he'd hit something. It wasn't big and it certainly wasn't clever, but it kept us entertained.

Well, imagine my surprise when, as the Brazilian chauffeur began to manoeuvre his way out of the car park, an almighty thud rattled the back of the van. The immediate giggling that erupted from behind made it instantly clear that no collision had taken place, other than that between years of juvenile British hijinks and the sophisticated ways of these classy gents from the Continent and beyond. They say football is a universal language but that day I found that comedy bridged the gaps pretty well too. I'm still annoyed with myself that I didn't hold an inquest and find out who the culprit was. Such super cool superstars, I'd find it hard to believe that any of them would've stooped to the ways of us English louts.

During our time in Brazil, I found one of these seven

to be arguably the most suave, debonair character I've ever encountered. Collar turned up on his leather jacket, sunglasses on at all times, Zinedine Zidane is the embodiment of a modern superstar – think James Dean with a French accent. He received by far the most attention out of all of us throughout the course of our stay and I felt compelled to tell him (via agent and translator), 'I've been watching you these past few days and you really are super cool.' He responded with an understated nod but no hint of an ego.

This coolness isn't an affectation, it's just the way he is. It was evident when he played too, unrivalled in his composure and nerve. Take his goal against Bayer Leverkusen for Real Madrid in the 2002 Champions League final, for example. Roberto Carlos bursts down the left wing, chasing a lofted pass, and hopefully hooks it back over his shoulder. It hangs in the air for what must seem like a lifetime to Zidane, waiting patiently on the edge of the box. As it starts to fall from the floodlit sky he raises his leg until it is perpendicular to his body and with one vicious swipe he arrows the ball beyond the reach of the German keeper. It's a great goal if you score it down the park with your pals, but to pull it off in a Champions League final with the scores tied is almost superhuman.

This wasn't a one-off for Zizou, either. Four years earlier in the Stade de France, he stole the show in his first World Cup final appearance (his next was admittedly less successful!). Facing the favourites Brazil in his homeland, Zidane scored two goals – both bullet headers from corner kicks – in the first 45 minutes to send the French on their way to victory. I might have been less inclined to rank him as high as eighth had he scored a third to claim only the second ever World Cup final hat-trick (my grandson got in touch at full-time to congratulate me on my then 32-year record!) but I fear my reasons for bumping him down would have been pretty transparent.

Goal scoring was just one small part of this near-complete player. He was a powerful athlete with the deftest of touches and the combination was devastating. When the ball fell to him in midfield (or anywhere, for that matter) his opponents were under a serious and constant threat of embarrassment. The way he commanded the ball, it was as though he was controlling the laws of physics. Players would lunge in to challenge him, only to realise that he'd already lifted the ball over their head. By the time they'd had the chance to turn around, the ball had fallen like lead to his toe and he'd made his getaway.

He was a supreme talent who shone regardless of the quality of teammate or opposition, excelling as the standout star for Bordeaux and later as the distinguished leader in a Galáctico-filled Real Madrid side. His time in between these two glittering spells was, however, the most interesting and formative period in his career.

He signed for Juventus in the summer of 1996, shortly after the Bianconeri had been crowned champions of Europe for only the second time in their history. Though he had been recruited on the back of his attacking performances for Bordeaux, his new bosses in Italy saw his role lying much deeper than he'd been used to, almost as a holding midfielder. Given the regard in which he is now held, this might seem like a huge waste of attacking talent, but lining up alongside Alessandro Del Piero, Christian Vieri, Didier Deschamps and Antonio Conte was only ever likely to improve him as a player.

After biding his time in the deeper role for half a season or so, he was given a chance further up the pitch and instantly began to blossom. His first season ended with mixed emotions, as Juventus won Serie A but lost in the Champions League final to Borussia Dortmund. That summer, with

Zidane having proven his attacking worth, the club brought in Edgar Davids to fill the defensive midfield role, allowing the Frenchman to play with more freedom.

During his time with Bordeaux it had been said that for all his swaggering confidence on the pitch, Zidane could be lacking in self-belief. Though many may struggle to believe this, it is the same impression I got when meeting him – there's an unmistakable shyness there. This is fine off the pitch, charming even, but on the pitch it is something which needs to be overcome. Within one season he had proven himself to the doubters of Turin. He had been all but written off by the locals within the first few months, only to become one of the biggest names in European football, prompting Real Madrid to come calling in 2001. This should act as the ultimate cautionary tale when it comes to judging new signings too quickly.

For all his achievements and the countless show-stealing performances, it was the greatest shame that his career had to end in the way it did, with that infamous headbutt on Marco Materazzi in the 2006 World Cup final. Yet even after that momentary loss of composure, I'm almost certain that it wasn't Mr Supercool who banged on the van.

7. BOBBY CHARLTON

One thing that is completely unavoidable when writing a book like this is the number of unsolicited opinions it generates. It stirs up something within people, a need to get their idols and favourite players recognised. Some of the suggestions I received were very helpful, both in challenging and reaffirming my view (I feel I should thank my wife Judith here for the many learned contributions she made throughout!). Naturally, for every useful comment that others made there were four or five of lesser quality. Yet the man whose opinion I turned to most was someone I didn't even consult while putting this book together.

Throughout my career I was always eager to learn from those more experienced than me, those who had knowledge to pass on. When I broke into the England set-up, I was no stranger to playing with top-class individuals – I trained with Bobby Moore and Martin Peters every day, after all – but I had never played alongside anyone who was genuinely world-famous. On overseas trips, even when Mooro was in his pomp, it was Bobby Charlton's signature that everybody wanted. He was the golden boy for England and Manchester United and in particularly far-flung places, the words 'Bobby' and 'Charlton' were often the only English people knew.

His travels with both club and country, in an age before 24-hour football coverage, meant that he'd been privileged enough to have seen more of the greats than pretty much anyone in the game. He had played against them too, often coming out on top, but the value I placed on Bobby's opinion is a result of more than just first-hand experience.

He was widely regarded as the greatest player in the world when we lifted the trophy in 1966, so when he spoke of those who influenced him you couldn't help but take note. To impress the best, you had to be doing something right. As a result, names such as Puskás and Di Stéfano were elevated to near godlike status and stars such as Roger Byrne and Tommy Taylor, victims of the Munich disaster whom he rated so highly, well, one can only imagine what impact they might have had on the English game.

A question often put to me and the rest of the 1966 World Cup-winning squad is which England player (if any) in the years since would have improved that team. Having thought long and hard about this, my answer would be Bryan Robson. This isn't to say that he would have been plugging a gap, because I firmly believe that there was not a weak spot in that side. Instead it's recognition of the fact that he was one of the few players who had the ability and attitude required to win a World Cup. One thing's for sure, his inclusion certainly would not have been at the expense of Bobby Charlton, because there hasn't been a better English midfielder than Bobby.

Bobby often stole the show with his ferocious shots from distance, but the finer details of his game are what have stuck with me years later, his control in particular. I'm not sure I've seen a more two-footed player in my life. His brother Jack used to say that even he wasn't sure which foot was his strongest, even in childhood. The ball just sat so comfortably at his feet that he never needed to shift it on to the other and this made him a constant threat.

It seems rather apt to take Jack's opinions from childhood into consideration, because I could fully believe that a kick-around with Bobby would have been a sight to behold even then. In fact, playing against him growing up probably went some way to making a World Cup-winning centre half out of Jack.

As is so often said of the great players, you only really understand how much of an impact they made when they're no longer there to make it. Players like Bobby manage to influence so much without people even realising, with subtle acts such as running down blind alleys to clear space for teammates or intentionally slowing down games to get a foothold. They make the game easier for those around them, often without acknowledgement.

In Bobby's case this was never more apparent than in the 1970 World Cup quarter-final against, you guessed it, West Germany. Those boys had a habit of being present for the most memorable moments of my career, both the highs and the lows. With less than half an hour on the clock I was pretty confident that I could chalk that particular matchup as one for the highs column, but then things began to unravel.

At 2-0 down, Franz Beckenbauer unsurprisingly started wandering further and further up the pitch and before long he was shooting on sight. In the 68th minute, with a shuffle of his feet he burst past Alan Mullery and onto the edge of our box before lashing a shot low towards Peter Bonetti's goal. In an uncharacteristic moment of error, the ball slipped under Peter's outstretched body and into the back of the net. A goal almost from nowhere; suddenly doubt started to spread throughout the ranks.

This was the first World Cup where tactical substitutions had been allowed. Bobby was 32 at the time and had run himself into the ground for over an hour. With our lead cut to just one goal, Sir Alf was faced with a big decision and one he needed to make quickly in order to halt the German fightback. Wary of Bobby's ageing legs, he was keen to ensure that he was rested whenever possible to preserve his creative energies. As had been the case in the previous game against Czechoslovakia, the decision was made to bring on a younger replacement. Up stepped Colin Bell to help us try to stop the onslaught. Just over five minutes later Uwe Seeler equalised and in the second period of extra time Gerd Müller scored the winner.

As I say, this decision wasn't an easy one for Sir Alf. The weather conditions alone were testing, as was the task of nullifying Beckenbauer's forays forwards. He had marked his German counterpart out of the final in '66 but this time around, Bobby's fourth World Cup, it was perhaps just one step too far. Of course, we can never know whether we would have won had he stayed on, and to suggest that Colin Bell's inclusion weakened the team is just patently unfair. The viewpoint peddled by many in the aftermath was that the substitution lost the match, but as Bobby himself has repeatedly pointed out over the years, the comeback had already started when he exited the field of play.

One thing we knew before the match had concluded, indeed years before that match came along, was that when Bobby eventually made way in the centre of England's midfield, it would take more than just one man to replace him. In truth, I'm not sure we have yet.

It is much to Bobby's credit that the hole he would soon leave was recognised long before he had stopped playing, both for club and country. He remains England's all-time top scorer to this day with 49 goals in 106 games and as an attacking midfielder no less, the sort of stats I can really appreciate. Truly world class and boasting a level of natural talent that England has never bettered, Bobby Charlton is one of the all-time greats by any nation's measure.

6. CRISTIANO RONALDO

He's come a long way from his early days at Manchester United as a skinny little trickster. A near-complete overhaul of approach, mentality and even physique have contributed to Cristiano Ronaldo transforming from a show pony with a penchant for diving to one of the most formidable attacking talents the sport has ever seen. His rise is one that should be studied by any budding footballer.

The majority of the players included in this book looked to be on the cusp of greatness from the very start and simply improved and progressed continually throughout their career. Cristiano Ronaldo was undoubtedly a hugely talented player from an early age, but his ascent to the very top was far from assured. He is a product of unrivalled dedication and intense training.

He first came to the attention of big-spenders Manchester United in a pre-season friendly against Sporting Lisbon. Sir Alex Ferguson's star names travelled to the Estádio José Alvalade as part of a pre-season tour which had seen them win four out of four in the USA. They were about to be humbled, and impressively so.

In the twentieth minute Ronaldo fired his first warning shot, stinging the palms of the distinguished Fabien Barthez. He went on to set up two goals while dazzling defenders with his extravagant dribbling and incisive runs. Sporting won 3-1, conceding only an own goal, and a beaten Ferguson set about acquiring their star man. An eighteen-year-old replacement for the recently departed David Beckham had just fallen into their lap (for a cool £12.24 million).

His debut season in England was eye-catching, though he stuttered in parts. His ability was plain to see but he too often nullified his threat with an over-indulgent stream of step-overs or feigning contact and injury where there was none. It was frustrating for all, not least me, to see such a talent tainted by the uglier parts of the game. Serious questions were raised about his potential, with many wondering whether he would ever become the reliable right winger that Manchester United craved or if his shortcomings would prove insurmountable.

The following season, in 2004/05, there was a notable effort to reduce the playacting. Ferguson spoke publicly about the steps they'd taken, saying, 'The part that we really worked hard on with him was not to overplay getting fouls. He has improved a lot on that. We said with your courage you don't need to do that.' Though this was all true – he had improved and there really was no need for it – he still displayed a tendency to revert to his old tactics when games started to go against him.

It was not until the 2006/07 season that Ronaldo finally started to show signs of becoming a true world-beater. With three seasons having passed since their last league title, the pressure was mounting on all at Old Trafford to end the drought. They started strongly and spent almost the entire season occupying the top spot, but Ronaldo's influence grew and grew as the season progressed. Facing three games in a week over the Christmas period, he scored a brace in each game as Man United claimed maximum points. Ronaldo finished the season as joint top scorer with 23 in all competitions and his side finished the season as champions. In many ways it was his breakthrough season, his coming of age.

His development as a player was mirrored by his physique, as his once narrow shoulders and spindly legs began to take a more muscular shape. Countless hours of gym work had enabled Ronaldo to rely on more than just pace and trickery to beat his man. His playing style became more direct as a result, beginning to drive towards goal as opposed to meekly jinking his way down the wing.

Having asserted himself as the star man at Old Trafford, the following season he set his sights a little higher. Despite taking until the last days of September to score his first league goal, he went on to dwarf his previous season's strike rate, scoring almost double with 42 in all competitions (31 in

the league). No longer simply a winger, he was fast becoming the complete attacking player. His goals powered Manchester United to a second consecutive league title and also to their first Champions League final in nine years, against Chelsea in Moscow. He scored in a 1-1 draw as they won courtesy of a now-famous John Terry slip and mishit in the shootout.

Ronaldo's first Champions League medal capped a season of countless accolades. He finished the year as top scorer in the Premier League, the Champions League and claimed the European Golden Shoe as the player to have scored the most goals across all the major European leagues. At the turn of the year he received further acknowledgement, claiming the prestigious Ballon d'Or as Europe's player of the year. This honour was heightened further by the fact that Lionel Messi was runner-up. As the two outstanding talents in world football, close scrutiny and comparison was inevitable and when Messi pipped him to the award the following year a topsy-turvy battle for supremacy began.

Having more than adequately replaced Beckham at Old Trafford, Cristiano Ronaldo had also set about toppling him as the world's most marketable footballer. With his off-field reputation matching his success on it, and with his name and number guaranteeing riches from shirt sales, he ticked all the boxes for a prospective Real Madrid signing and once he became their top transfer target it seemed inevitable that he'd be leaving England.

Few eyebrows were raised when on 26 June 2009 he sealed a record-breaking move to the Santiago Bernabéu. At £80 million, the deal comfortably usurped the previous record of £56 million which Madrid had also stumped up for Milan's Kaká, earlier that same month. Astronomical figures, but no less than we'd come to expect from the club that gave us the Galácticos.

They had joined a team very much in a state of transition. A whole host of big-name players including Arjen Robben, Ruud Van Nistelrooy, Wesley Sneijder and Fabio Cannavaro had all departed the Bernabéu that summer to make room for Ronaldo and company, so the task was daunting to say the least. Nonetheless, the clear-out meant that there was plenty of opportunity for new heroes to present themselves. Kaká struggled to recapture the form of his Milan days, partly due to niggling long-standing injuries, but Ronaldo had no such problems. The success that followed was emblematic of the man.

In the media cauldron of Madrid it takes a confident personality to flourish and one thing Ronaldo has never been accused of is lacking self-belief. On the pitch, Real Madrid needed not only to improve their own game, but to find a way to stop their arch-rivals Barcelona who were enjoying something of a purple patch. In fact, Barcelona were being widely described as one of the greatest teams in history.

Ronaldo settled immediately, scoring five times in his first four league matches, and this strike rate barely slipped over the course of the season. He notched up 26 goals in just 29 league appearances and finished up as the club's top scorer in all competitions with 33. This was not however enough to lead the side to glory, as two league defeats against Barcelona proved to be the difference, and Real Madrid missed out on the title by just three points. The fact that Lionel Messi also managed to outscore him with 34 in the league and 47 in all competitions was further evidence of the size of the obstacle standing between Madrid and ultimate success.

The following season saw Ronaldo improve further still, scoring an astonishing 40 times in the league, nine more than Messi, though in terms of trophies the story didn't change. A four-point gap separated the two teams at the end of the season, thanks largely to Barcelona's devastating 5-0 El Clásico victory in the November.

In 2012, at the end of his third season in Madrid, Ronaldo finally got the chance to taste victory in La Liga and with relative comfort too, amassing a huge points total of 100, nine more than Barcelona and a whopping 39 more than third-placed Valencia. By this stage his strike rate across all three seasons actually exceeded a goal per game, something which he has maintained at the time of writing two years later.

Though it is undoubtedly easier to score when you're playing for a team like Madrid or Barcelona who will control and dominate games, this almost mechanical consistency is hugely impressive. It takes a certain mentality to not ease off when you're winning comfortably but Ronaldo refuses to rest while there are still goals to be scored. This is all the more impressive when compared to his first flamboyant footsteps in English football. Gone are (most of) the histrionics, the diving, the excessive showboating and countless runs down blind alleys, and what's left is one of the most potent attacking forces the game has ever seen.

5. ALFREDO DI STÉFANO

Obviously I'm not the first person in history to try to rank the greats and undoubtedly I won't be the last. In a game all about winning and naming champions, it's part of our nature as players and fans to want to decide who's the greatest. As a result, I'm able to call upon the views of those best placed to judge certain individuals, including countrymen and teammates who've had their say over the years. Given the subjective nature of the task, I found this to be as distracting as it was helpful.

While I was working on this book, the life of one of the undisputed greats came to an end. Alfredo Di Stéfano died on 7 July 2014 having lived an astoundingly full life. The catalyst in Real Madrid's meteoric growth and the proud representative of no fewer than three national sides, his story is enough to fill a book all on its own. The sadness of his passing, midway through a South American World Cup, was tempered by the overwhelming wave of respect and the tributes that followed.

Aged 88, having enjoyed his footballing heyday in the 1950s and 60s, those who can remember the world of football before Alfredo Di Stéfano are now in the minority. It was a time when club football was a world away from the international arena it is today.

A question often asked of me is 'Who did you try to play like growing up?', and the truth is no one and everyone. You add what you can to your game, learning from the stars of the time, but it's rare that you'll find one player who can provide a blueprint for your game. But by all accounts, Di Stéfano was the blueprint for every outfield position, the original total footballer, someone whom every player could learn from. In the days after Di Stéfano's death, one of the most telling tributes came from Diego Maradona who said, 'For me he was a master, he taught me a lot of things. I am reminded about him during many moments and the truth is that all of football is in mourning today because a true great has died.' He wasn't alone in expressing this sentiment either.

Pelé had his say on Di Stéfano back in 2009, going one further than Maradona by saying, 'People argue between Pelé or Maradona. For me, Di Stéfano is the best. He was much more complete.' Though bold, this statement is far from outlandish. His achievements in club football are unrivalled: five European Cups, eight Spanish league titles, four Colombian league titles and two Argentinian league titles, in addition to a number of domestic and intercontinental cups. As the leader in each team he played for, this mountain of silverware is evidence of his prowess as a team player, while his two European Player of the Year trophies and his tally of 307 goals for Real Madrid put his individual ability beyond doubt.

The case for Di Stéfano is certainly compelling. I think it's safe to say that there's little more he could have done over the course of his career to play himself into contention for that top spot, and indeed his legacy probably outweighs that of any player before or since. But was he really the greatest?

For me, he was both a victim and a beneficiary of the time in which he played. On the one hand, there was so much uncharted territory in the sport, so many trails to be blazed. Professional football was still establishing itself in the decades after the Second World War and European club football was set to become the springboard for success for footballers the world over. Di Stéfano's impact upon the sport was so great that it almost counts against him, however illogically, as his inspired approach to the game led to such widespread improvement in the standard of play and, by comparison, the players he came up against were weaker. This underlines the supreme difficulty in ranking players from different eras and in Di Stéfano's case you have to make an exception, considering his legacy jointly with his ability.

For all his success, it seems strange to think that he was something of a late bloomer. In 1945, at the age of nineteen, he had yet to cement his place in the first team at River Plate and was sent out on loan to Huracán to gain experience.

When you consider that the likes of Pelé, Maradona and Cruyff were the stars of their respective teams and even their national sides by the age of seventeen, seeing your twenties in with what could at best be described as an educational loan spell doesn't sound like the path to world domination. Di Stéfano was just biding his time.

Two years later, having flourished at Huracán before returning to lead River Plate to a league title, he began his brief stint with the Argentinian national side. The first chapter in the most curious of stories, Di Stéfano's experiences of international football were interrupted by a whole host of non-footballing matters. As was soon to become typical of Di Stéfano, his short spell with Argentina was resoundingly triumphant. Six games in the Copa América saw him score six times and lift the trophy. A 100 per cent record. Over the course of his career he would also represent Spain and Colombia at international level, but sadly he never appeared at a World Cup, missing out on Chile '62 with Spain due to a late injury.

Back with River Plate, the following season was put on hold as a players' strike halted football across the country. With his hand forced, Di Stéfano headed north to Colombia. The domestic league was also in flux with a rebel league being formed, breaking away from FIFA in what would later come to be known as the El Dorado years (1949–54), the golden era.

Di Stéfano signed for the Millonarios Fútbol Club in Bogotá and it didn't take long for him to make an impact. He won the league title in his first season and would do so twice more while top-scoring in 1951 and 1952. In the year of his third Colombian title, Millonarios were invited to play in a tournament marking the 50th anniversary of Spanish giants Real Madrid. With Spanish scouts watching on, Di

Stéfano's performance set the clock ticking on his time in Colombia – the only question was who would win the race to sign him.

A fierce battle ensued between Real Madrid and Barcelona – one that makes Figo's switch between the two look like an amicable arrangement – with General Franco allegedly weighing in to help sway the contest. Barcelona initially believed that they had signed him from River Plate, but the players' dispute and his consequent move to Millonarios cast doubt on the deal. When Di Stéfano finally put pen to paper with their bitter rivals, Real Madrid president Santiago Bernabéu (after whom their stadium is now named) was recognised as the instrumental figure in securing his signature for Los Merengues.

By the time Di Stéfano arrived in Madrid expectations had risen considerably as a result and so, with Barcelona still bemoaning the injustices of his move, he set to work on proving that the battle had been worth fighting. He couldn't have got off to a better start.

It had been 21 years since Madrid had last won a league title but in his first season Di Stéfano led them to victory, seemingly opening the floodgates of success. He was 27 at the time of his move so it would have been natural to expect that he was nearing his peak, but in retrospect he was just getting started. Over the next four seasons he picked up three more league winner's medals (he won eight in total in his time with the club) but oddly it was the 1955/56 season, one which saw Madrid return to the lowly third place which they had been used to, that is considered one of the most important in their history.

Away from Spanish domestic football, the inaugural campaign of a new competition was taking place. Pitting the heavyweights from the best leagues in Europe against one another, the European Cup introduced a level of glamour and prestige never before seen in club football. With their focus split, Madrid prioritised the European competition, a move which raised the profile of the club to levels previously unimaginable.

Victory in the first ever European Cup final against France's Stade de Reims brought untold rewards to the Spanish capital, not least the chance to host the decider the following year. As it happened, success bore more success and Madrid would successfully defend their crown against Fiorentina in front of more than 120,000 fans. What's more, this time around they wouldn't be so sloppy as to let their league form suffer as a result. Nor would they the following season, their dominion over club football growing ever more imposing.

By the end of the 1950s, in the six short years since Di Stéfano's arrival, Real Madrid had grown from Spain's third or fourth best club side into the world's undisputed champions. Lifting the first five European Cups left the sort of indelible impression on the world of football that no multi-million pound marketing campaign or stadium revamp ever could. Alfredo Di Stéfano was the key to this. A player with the determination to break the status quo and the ability to achieve it, he was a star, a leader and a team player all rolled into one revolutionary man.

I read many of the obituaries and tributes to Di Stéfano when the news broke in July. One line kept appearing, having caught the eye of countless journalists as indeed it did mine. Speaking of his youth in Barracas, Buenos Aires, not far from where the English first introduced the sport to Argentina, Di Stéfano said that he learned how to play in 'the academy of the streets', enjoying free-for-all games which went on late into the night. It's somehow comforting to think that Di Stéfano, who ultimately progressed to become a professor of the sport, began his footballing days just like the rest of us, kicking a ball about in the street.

4. LIONEL MESSI

For two decades every single young, talented, attack-minded Argentinian was weighted down by the same formidable tag: 'the next Maradona'. His passion-fuelled and exuberant approach was such a comprehensive representation of the nation's psyche that he was seen as the perfect Argentinian player, the fan on the pitch. These are not unrealistic qualities to want to see in a player, but comparisons to Maradona inevitably call for much more than mere passion. When you factor in his extraordinary footballing ability, coupled with his heroics in the blue and white shirt, they combine to form the most unattainable of expectations. Even the great man himself may have felt a slight twinge of fear at the task in hand.

A handful of notable players managed to shake off the tag to forge a successful career, such as Ariel Ortega and Carlos Tevez, but these players are firmly in the minority. For every Ortega there is a long line of hapless failures, those who found the pressure to be inescapable. In October of 2004, the next dutiful carrier of the Maradona burden made his debut for Barcelona; one Lionel Messi. Though much anticipated by those close to the Catalonian club, his introduction to top-flight football was relatively low-key. Having shone throughout his rapid ascent up the age groups of the club's famed youth set-up, first team coach Frank Rijkaard was keen to look after the budding talent.

A steady couple of seasons followed, predominantly consisting of sparkling cameos, and so by the time the 2006 World Cup rolled around he was still far from the global icon he is today. So much so that when, as part of a media event arranged by McDonald's, I was introduced to the scruffy little teenager I had little idea who he was. Hair down to his shoulders, wearing jeans and a jean jacket with some worn-out trainers, he just didn't look like a modern footballer, though I was assured he was.

He didn't act like one either. There was no hint of the ego that you might reasonably expect of a wunderkind playing for Barcelona and Argentina. Almost childlike, he only seemed at ease when one of the event organisers sourced a football for him. With the absent-minded ease that one might flip a coin, he sat on the floor, feet stretched out before him, and began to play keepie-uppie with the ball. Nobody had asked him to, it wasn't a party trick, but I found myself watching as he lazily juggled the ball.

Messi played a bit-part role in the tournament, the highlight of which was his first World Cup goal coming in the 6-0 rout of Serbia and Montenegro, but he was on his way to becoming the hottest name in world football. When he returned to Barcelona, his stock having risen as a result of his solid performances at the finals, Rijkaard was ready to use him rather more liberally in the first team. This was in no small part due to the calls for his inclusion from fans at the Nou Camp who had been thoroughly impressed by his appearances to date.

A strong start to the season was interrupted by a three-month injury lay-off, but in March 2007 he put in his first top-class performance. Barcelona vs. Real Madrid in the

Nou Camp. El Clásico. A game which has humbled the most experienced of stars, and with heavyweights such as Raúl, Ruud Van Nistelrooy and Samuel Eto'o vying for the headlines, the world was bound to take note when a nineteen-year-old stole the show.

With Real Madrid taking the initiative, Messi had twice needed to drag Barcelona onto a level footing with two emphatic equalisers, but a Sergio Ramos header midway through the second half appeared to have put the game beyond the home side. That was until the 90th minute when Messi, snatching a hopeful Ronaldinho through ball away from a huddle of players, outstripped a flat-footed Madrid defence before smashing the ball beyond Iker Casillas. A goal from nothing to round off the first El Clásico hat-trick for fifteen years. It was the goal that promoted him from his wunderkind status to that of undisputed star.

At once, the comparisons to Maradona began to rain down in torrents. This time it was hard to mark it down as mere wishful thinking and over the coming months and seasons the similarities only seemed to become more apparent. Having come to be widely recognised as one of the world's greatest talents, fans had grown used to seeing him score goals that Maradona would have been proud of but in April 2007, against Getafe in the semi-final of the Copa del Rey (the Spanish cup), he scored a goal that Maradona had scored before. It pushed the similarities between the two players from the realms of coincidence into the downright uncanny.

The goal was an almost exact recreation of Maradona's 'Goal of the Century', the high-speed long-distance dribble and finish against England in 1986. Messi's goal began by receiving the ball just inside his own half, on the right-hand side, just as Maradona had more than twenty years previously in Mexico. He shook off two men before accelerating into the opposition's half. Alternating between a long-striding canter and tiptoed close control, he advanced at pace towards and then into the Getafe box. At this point in the move, you have to start to wonder whether Messi was deliberately trying to replicate Maradona's most famous goal.

Before a commentator or supporter even gets a chance to point out the resemblance, Messi slips past the grounded keeper before placing the ball beyond the last man who is still desperately scampering back on to the line. A carbon copy, from start to finish.

For one country to produce two players capable of scoring such a goal is impressive enough, but for both players to actually score it is bordering on unbelievable.

The goal represented a watershed moment in Messi's career. It gave the people, both media and fans, exactly what they wanted and in a manner more perfect than they could ever have hoped for. It made clear once and for all that Messi was not just the latest in a long line of 'next Maradonas', he was the real thing, a worthy successor. At club level at least.

When the 2014 World Cup in Brazil finally arrived, four years of endless talking neared an end. It was seen by journalists in Argentina and throughout the world as the chance Messi had been waiting for to cement his legacy on the world stage. The line in the sand was drawn. 'Everything is in his favour, if he can't even play like Maradona in a South American World Cup then how can we speak of him in the same breath?' This mantra was repeated ad infinitum by the world's press.

The gnashing of teeth from the world's press that greeted him in Brazil was of course unfair, but his performances still represent a fascinating case study. They also highlight the differences between Messi and Maradona, not necessarily weaknesses on either's part.

The group stages were supposedly going to be a walkthrough for Argentina. They did eventually finish top with maximum points, but relied upon sensational strikes from Messi in all three games, including a wondrous curling effort in the final minutes against Iran to avoid an unlikely draw. So far so good for Messi, though his team's stuttering start was cause for concern.

His four goals by this point saw that he'd bettered Maradona's goal tally from the 1982 World Cup and was one shy of his total when he'd led Argentina to victory in 1986. It was growing increasingly clear, however, that goals alone weren't going to satisfy the critics. He was expected to replicate Maradona's leadership from '86 too. And so he did, providing a defence-splitting assist for Ángel Di María's winner against Switzerland in the first knockout round, before stepping up to score Argentina's first penalty to set them on their way to victory in a shootout against the Netherlands. Team play, bullish leadership and goals. He'd stepped up when needed, but the bar was rising all the while.

In Argentina and Germany, the final pitted two teams against one another that many had tipped to go all the way, but the attitudes towards the two sides could not have been more different. Many dubbed it Germany vs. Messi, and that seemed to be how it was judged. If Argentina lost then Messi had failed, but if Germany won it was victory for the world's form team. Of course Argentina did lose on the night and as Messi picked up his Golden Ball trophy (admittedly not the standout choice as winner) it was clear to see that he felt he'd failed.

It has to be remembered that failure for Messi means something completely different to failure for the rest of us. Even if Argentina had managed to win on the night, if Messi hadn't been the star player he would still have been compared disparagingly to Maradona. Even if he'd been Man of the Match, his critics would have pointed to the fact that he hadn't scored a goal as good as Maradona's Goal of the Century en route to victory. There comes a point where you have to look at Messi as Messi and not the next Maradona, when you count up his three Champions League winner's medals and compare them to Maradona's nil, or look at how Messi has already beaten Maradona's goal tally for Argentina and has long since passed his career tally at club level with years still to play.

Of course I don't say this to discount Maradona's achievements in front of goal or in European club competition, but rather to acknowledge that the circumstances dictate these records. They're different players in different teams in different eras, and Maradona's achievements shouldn't count against Messi. There comes a time when we accept that Messi will not eventually become Maradona, in the same way that he did not become Pelé. He is forging a separate route to greatness and we should just be thankful to have witnessed two players capable of scoring that same sublime goal.

3. DIEGO ARMANDO MARADONA

Football is a tribal game full of partisan allegiances, so it should come as no surprise that a number of the great players included in this book have their detractors. Yet when it comes to Diego Maradona it's somewhat different. The strength of feeling on both sides of the fence is unlike that for any other player. It's not simply a matter of who he played for or how he played the game, and it's more than a question of taste. The list of successes and achievements that he racked up throughout his eventful career is comparable to any of the greats in the history of the game, but his list of misdemeanours is of a similar length. Divisive in every sense.

Of course I'm not blind to Maradona's abilities; few players have ever displayed the explosive dribbling skills or match-winning ability that came so easily to him. It's taken nearly 30 years to find someone who even comes close, in Lionel Messi. But for me greatness requires more than just playing the game really, really well. It's about the way that you play it, whether you can maintain your principles and accept defeat within the terms and spirit of the laws of football, as opposed to bending or breaking them in order to snatch victory. As we all know, Maradona does not conform to this definition of greatness. But as I say, when it comes to Diego Maradona, it's different.

So for me, a proud Englishman who witnessed both his genius and his deviousness in the flesh, I feel it necessary to enlist the views of those who sit firmly on his side of the fence to better inform my opinion. Who better to ask then than two of his former teammates, Ricardo 'Ricky' Villa and Osvaldo 'Ossie' Ardiles? Now these are two players whom I greatly admire, and who understand both the English and Argentine mentality better than anyone, so there are few men more qualified to judge. Their answer was simple – 'Compared to him, we are ordinary mortals.'

This is the sort of praise that has rained down on Maradona for decades, but that's from fans, press, people who have never measured themselves against him in a professional capacity. Footballers have egos, as we all know, and to be so self-effacing requires something special. I got a glimpse of this something special in that game in 1986. Standing among the crowd, surrounded by fans of all nations – as unbiased a jury as you could possibly assemble – unanimous verdicts were reached on both of his key interventions.

The first came just over five minutes into the second half. Maradona, having forced his way onto the edge of the English penalty area, laid the ball off to Jorge Valdano and burst into the box. Almost magnetically, after Valdano had clumsily sent the ball spinning into the air and England's Steve Hodge had aimlessly swatted it away with his left boot, the ball came floating back towards Argentina's unmistakable number 10. Peter Shilton rushed from his line and the chance slipped away from Maradona. Or so I thought.

With Shilton's height advantage of six or seven inches and with his arms fully outstretched it seemed impossible that he would lose out in the aerial challenge. From my position in the stands, in line with the linesman and a good 30 yards from the touchline, I watched as Maradona did away with the rulebook. It's one of the most famous goals in history and it's one which should never have stood. As he leapt and punched the ball past Shilton, the fans surrounding me leapt too. 'Handball!' boomed out from all around, but to no avail. The linesman and referee had been duped. A combination of disbelief and outrage swelled, sweeping throughout the Estadio Azteca, save for the swathes of jubilant albiceleste. Shilton and co. protested in vain as Maradona orchestrated contrived celebrations.

Cynical and unsportsmanlike, it represented what's wrong with the game in one concise episode. It was an unforgiveable act, yet here I am ranking him as the third greatest player of all time. This is purely a testament to his ability – he's in third place in spite of his approach to the game – because when the ball was at his feet there really was nobody better. Within five minutes of the incident which he later laughably described as 'The Hand of God', he scored a goal that really did have an air of divinity about it.

The most breathtaking dribbling display ever seen, concluded with the coolest of finishes, it has come to be widely known as the Goal of the Century. It's a goal which is seared into the mind of every football fan, lit by the whitish light of the blazing Mexican sun. From the point at which Maradona spins on the ball beside the centre circle (complete with its strange spider-shaped shadow) to the moment he scrambles to his feet to celebrate, having held off the challenges of no fewer than seven Englishmen, it's so firmly embedded in football history that I need not describe it in any greater detail.

This was a player at his very peak, a player who was determined to lead his side to glory and one whom very few were capable of stopping. It was no surprise then to see Argentina lift the trophy two games later. That 1986 team has since wrongly been described as a one-man team. The two Jorges for example – Valdano and Burruchaga – were both hugely talented players, but they knew their role within the team. That Argentina side was set up to let one man, the greatest in the world at the time, flourish – as opposed to leaving him to do all the work. In my view, this couldn't be further from a one-man team. In fact, it's exactly how a great team should operate, working to get the best out of one another. I assure you, no one-man team would ever manage to win a World Cup.

Even with the side built around him, Maradona's task was far from easy. It takes a great player to handle the responsibility that comes with being the focal point of a side, but this came naturally to him. Not just for Argentina, either. This was borne out in his spells with club sides in both Argentina and Europe. He maintained an average of just over one goal in every game at club level over the course of his career, having started at full tilt at his first club, Argentinos Junior, where he spent five years and scored over a century of goals.

He was prolific during his short spells at Boca Juniors and Barcelona, but it was for his time with Napoli that he has come to be best known. As with the Argentina team of 1986, though Maradona was the undisputed star, he was backed by a team of good, reliable professionals – including Ciro Ferrara and Salvatore Bagni who each amassed just shy of 50 caps for Italy. Yet unlike with Argentina who had won the World Cup in 1978 when Maradona was still just a promising kid, Napoli did not have a history of success. Prior to Maradona's arrival, two Coppa Italia wins were the only major honours in their entire history. Of course, that was all set to change.

The Naples club presented Maradona to a packed-out São Paulo stadium on 5 July 1984, with more than 70,000 fans turning up (the exact number varies depending on who you speak to) to get a glimpse of their new talisman. It quickly became clear that Maradona and the Napoli fans were going to get along. He was immediately met with the adoration of the fans that he felt had been so lacking during his time with Barcelona.

Progress on the pitch was steady. The club had finished twelfth out of sixteen teams in the season before his arrival so there was a lot of work to be done. Maradona's first season saw a marginal improvement with the side moving up to eighth, but the following year they jumped up to third. Momentum was beginning to build, Maradona was absolutely flying and after a brief summer break in Mexico – a World Cup winner's medal his only souvenir – he returned more determined than ever.

The affinity he found with the support in Napoli was akin to that which he held with those back in Argentina, the mentalities of the two groups almost indistinguishable. He had said upon his arrival, 'I want to be an idol to the poor children of Naples – they are as I was in Buenos Aires.' This feeling only seemed to grow. The events of the 1986/87 season saw him elevated far beyond idol status, viewed almost as a deity throughout the city as he powered the club to their first Scudetto in their history. With such historical northern dominance in Serie A, a win for the southern side represented more than just sporting success. It was tribal and fierce, with Naples viewing itself almost as a republic and Maradona as their leader.

Napoli were keen to prove that this triumph was more than just a perfect storm but their competition had started to strengthen. Napoli fought strongly to retain their title in 1988 but rearguard action proved decisive as AC Milan claimed the title on the final day, having conceded only fourteen times in 30 games. A disappointing end to the season, but the Neapolitan faithful could only have dreamt of a second place finish before Maradona. The following year they continued to build upon their reputation as a serious challenger, finishing second once again in 1988/89, this time to another Milanese side in Inter Milan.

The 1989/90 championship carried an added distinction as it preceded Italia '90, a World Cup on home soil. Serie A was the strongest league in world football at the time, boasting players of the calibre of Marco Van Basten, Rudi Voller, Lothar Matthäus, Roberto Baggio and, of course, Diego Maradona. All eyes on Italy.

Maradona scored sixteen times as Napoli collected their second Scudetto in four years. Given the formidable opposition they faced, this feat was made all the more impressive by Maradona's visible weight gain and stories of him missing training sessions. Fitness and punctuality were never central to his success; instead he was driven by pure passion and determination. Nonetheless, these warning signs would culminate in a failed drug test and a lengthy ban in 1991.

Though starting to chug slightly, he still had enough in the tank to play a leading role in Italia '90. Having conquered Italy at club level, he was not about to throw away the opportunity to do so in an international capacity. Following a shock defeat to Cameroon and a draw against Romania, Argentina scraped out of their four-team group as one of the best third-placed teams. Having survived that scare, they began to liven up, seeing off rivals Brazil in the first knockout round before a penalty shootout victory against Yugoslavia landed them a place in the semi-finals. Their opponents? As if by script ...

In what would essentially prove to be Maradona's last hurrah, regarding both his time in Italy and his career as a whole, he couldn't have asked for more fitting circumstances. Despite facing the home nation, with Napoli's San Paolo stadium the venue, it was hard to tell which side the locals favoured. In the build-up to the fixture, Maradona called upon the Neapolitans to side with him over the nation from which they felt so detached. His message to them was simple: 'Naples is not Italy.' Spoken with the authority of a man who knew that all he need do was ask, it was enough to split the Azzurri support.

Argentina won the match on penalties before losing out in the final to West Germany, but the match in Naples would remain a vignette of Maradona's greatness. The story has been told again and again across the city in the decades since, as has that of his arrival in 1984 and of so many moments in between, each tale focusing in on his better qualities, the admirable features that endeared him to a loyal fan base. They highlight his bewildering ability to lead, to stir passions and get people on side, not excepting those seemingly allied to the opposition. Though it didn't half smart to be on the receiving end of it, especially when the rules fell victim in the process, you couldn't help but admire him when he played fair.

2. JOHAN CRUYFF

In the build-up to the 2014 World Cup in Brazil I found myself glued to the reruns of previous finals, the 1974 final in particular. West Germany and the Netherlands reigniting a fierce rivalry in Munich's iconic Olympiastadion, it was a game steeped in history.

Much like in '66 when he did battle with Bobby Charlton, the game saw Franz Beckenbauer pitted against another of the game's greats, Johan Cruyff. It didn't take long for the battle to erupt. Forty-five seconds had elapsed when the Dutchman picked up the ball in the centre circle. He ambled forward and with a shuffle of his feet burst past one German defender before being felled by a second. Penalty. Johan Neeskens held his nerve and a crowd of orange mobbed him in delight. The players returned to their half for the second kick-off in as many minutes.

As the cameraman tracks them from behind the German goal, one man stands out at the back of the pack. The number 14, captain's armband strapped to his bicep and palms downturned, pats the air, urging his teammates to keep calm. The calm assuredness that came so naturally to Cruyff was always evident, a hallmark of Total Football. Watching this back, 40 years on, I was reminded of another of his great assets.

His movement defied marking. Defenders didn't know whether to get tight or back off and even if they could decide, putting it into practice was a different matter altogether. It's not as though I had forgotten that he was a tricky little player but when players are revered to the degree that Cruyff is, it can be easy to take them for granted. While I opted for the full 90 minutes, it only takes the briefest glimpse at archive footage to be convinced of his impeccable control and balance – the man was quicksilver.

As it happens, the '74 final turned sour for Cruyff and the Dutch as West Germany came from behind to win 2-1, but his career is filled with examples of his talent and hard graft paying off. Cruyff was never prepared to settle. Even when playing alongside great players in successful teams, he would always want to push on and improve. This was in evidence from the very start of his career, which saw him quickly rise to the top of a talented youth set-up at Ajax to become a star of the first team within a couple of seasons.

Having grown up in the streets opposite Ajax's old De Meer Stadion, his sheer persistence was enough to get him noticed. His mother worked for the club and Johan would visit her each day on his lunch-break. He became such a familiar face around the place that the coaches allowed him to join in and soon he began to flourish. The transition from schoolboy to professional football was seamless, thanks in part to Ajax's scientific approach. Classrooms and blackboards were a staple of the Ajax way.

It showed in the way he played. His understanding of the game was unrivalled. Rinus Michels and his coaching team would ensure that Cruyff, like the rest of the squad, knew the requirements for every position so that Ajax could play in the most fluid of styles: Totaalvoetbal. When Cruyff broke into the first team, however, the club looked a long way off achieving anything remotely resembling fluid football.

In his debut season of 1964/65 the team finished thirteenth in the Eredivisie, the worst campaign in the club's professional history, but Cruyff's role in the team was noteworthy and set to grow. 1965 saw the appointment of a new manager, Rinus Michels, a returning forward who had clocked up over 200 appearances for the club. His influence over the club was transformative and wide-reaching – and it didn't take long to show.

The following season the Ajax blueprint started to take shape. With their home-grown starlet grabbing the headlines the team consigned the disappointment of the previous year to history. Cruyff got his first taste of success in the form of the Eredivisie title, scoring 25 goals in 23 games in league and cup. In later seasons Michels would encourage him to play from deeper, becoming a central cog in the team and not simply the prolific finisher.

Momentum continued to gather for the Amsterdam side as they won five of the next seven championships and lifted the Dutch Cup four times. With Ajax's dominance in the Netherlands strengthening all the while, they began to set their sights a little higher. Throughout the 1960s Real Madrid, AC Milan and Benfica were setting the pace in world football.

The European Cup was the ultimate test for Ajax; win and they could proudly stand alongside the Spanish, Italian and Portuguese powerhouses. Their first chance to do so came at the end of the 1968/69 season. Lining up against Milan in the Santiago Bernabéu for the final, the stage couldn't have been more prestigious. Cruyff was the recognised star of Dutch football by this time, having been named Dutch Player of the Year in consecutive years, but even he was powerless against a formidable Milan side. They lost 4-1 and chalked it up as a learning experience.

And learn they did. Two years later in 1971 they once again took their place in the European Cup final, this time held in Wembley Stadium. The opposition were Greece's Panathinaikos and there was to be no repeat of Ajax's humbling in Madrid. De Amsterdammers ran out 2-0 winners and brought the much coveted European Cup home to their already crowded trophy cabinet. It would stay there for some time too.

The victory undoubtedly played a part in the recognition Cruyff enjoyed as an individual that year, winning the Ballon d'Or as Europe's star performer and claiming his third Dutch Player of the Year award. Ajax had become the dominant force in European football. They held on to the star prize for two more seasons, overcoming Italian opposition in the successive finals, with Cruyff scoring twice to beat Inter Milan 2-0 in '72 and captaining the side to a 1-0 victory over Juventus in '73.

In the space of less than a decade, Ajax had gone from downbeat also-rans to the most successful club around. They weren't just grinding out results, either. The football was ground-breaking, with a tactical understanding more comprehensive than any side had displayed previously. The passing, the movement, it was beautiful; but Ajax were almost mechanical in their operation. The pioneering work of Rinus Michels from 1965 onwards became so deep-rooted within the club that when he left in '71, following the first European Cup triumph, the Romanian Stefan Kovács was able to step in and continue the good work without so much as a blip in form.

This would not have been possible, however, without Johan Cruyff at the heart of the team. He had taken on the teachings of Michels and had mastered his tactics. An obsessive will to improve saw him become an extension of his manager on the pitch, but in the years after Michels' departure he found the professionalism which had led them to glory beginning to wane. Despite the adulation he enjoyed from Ajax fans and the nation as a whole, Cruyff had grown discontented and sought a move to ensure complacency wouldn't infect him too. It was this drive that set him apart from his rivals, the type of unwavering determination that pushes good players on to greatness.

His next move was a natural choice, reuniting with Michels at Barcelona for a record fee, just under £1 million. Though one of Spain's biggest clubs, they hadn't won the title in thirteen years prior to his arrival but Cruyff and Michels needed little time to rediscover the winning formula from their days in Amsterdam. Dutch flair blended perfectly with Catalonian passion as one of the most famous seasons in the club's history unfolded.

Years of Madrid dominance had only acted to intensify the rivalry between the two clubs. Never afraid to stir up controversy, Cruyff further stoked the flames when declaring to the press that despite interest from Real he would never have chosen them over Barcelona due to their association with General Franco – a move that endeared him to fans of his new club as much as it turned the Madrid faithful against him.

Having secured his place in the spotlight, when Barcelona visited the Bernabéu to contest one of the most hotly anticipated El Clásicos in history, the pressure was on for the star man to shine. Yet while he was happy to court the attentions of the media away from the pitch, nothing could sway him from his unselfish approach. Pulling the strings in a dazzling team display, Cruyff scored once in a 5-0 demolition. It was the standout result in a glorious season which saw the Blaugranas finally crowned champions once again. The match rocked Madrid so much that a local newspaper led with the headline, 'Madrid in the hands of Barça. They were rag dolls.' A humbling even more thorough than Cruyff could have dreamt of.

1974 saw Cruyff at his peak. He ended the year as the European Footballer of the Year, but the role he played in ending Barcelona's La Liga drought was not the main event. This brings us almost full circle to that iconic final between the Netherlands and West Germany but there was one moment of complete genius, squeezed in between his league success and World Cup disappointment, that has since become the enduring image of Johan Cruyff's sensational career. The hallmark of brilliance.

In a first round group game, long before the heartbreak of the final, the Netherlands went up against Sweden in Dortmund's Westfalenstadion. The unfortunate man tasked with marking Cruyff, as much as anybody could mark someone from that 1974 Dutch side, was Jan Olsson.

On 23 minutes, with Olsson already showing signs of twisted blood, Cruyff began to toy with his victim. Taking receipt of a pinpoint cross-field pass from Arie Haan, Cruyff looked clumsy at first. The controlling touch was slightly heavy and the ball slipped away from him for a second. He reached out his leg to retrieve it, stepped on it and stumbled before regaining his balance. Olsson watched on, unaware that his chance to avoid humiliation had just slid from his grasp. The ball had been there for the taking for the briefest of moments. He could have prevented what was about to come but little did he know, little did any of us know, just what Cruyff was about to unleash on him.

As the two faced up to each other out in acres of space on the left wing, the Dutchman started to work the ball on to his right foot, seemingly preparing to whip in an inswinging cross. Then it happened.

While Olsson, his teammates and the other 50,000 or so spectators turned to look where the cross would land, Plan B was being put into action. Before Olsson even had a chance to realise what was happening, Cruyff flicked the ball back towards the byline with his instep, turning 180 degrees and accelerating into the space. The crowd celebrated as though a goal had been scored. Not just a tap-in either. When he did finally cross the move fizzled out but nobody seemed to care. The game finished 0-0 and yet still managed to become one of the most talked-about fixtures in tournament history, all for that moment of ingenuity.

The Cruyff Turn, as it came to be known throughout the world of football, is now a fairly regular sight on football pitches across the globe. Provided the player in control of the ball has the required skills of deception, it's the ideal move to create space and time where there is none. But before 1974 the move that seems almost rudimentary nowadays was almost unthinkable. Those who only had half an eye on the match at the time would have been left befuddled by how the two still shots, of Cruyff first shaping to cross and then of him wriggling away down the line, could possibly be pieced together.

It wasn't his most important achievement or even his most spectacular, but in that moment you can see exactly how Cruyff managed to assert himself as one of the greatest ever. Whether it was finding a way past a weary defender or leaving the club that had been his life for more than a decade, if he wasn't happy with a situation he would never settle; he would always find another way.

1. PELÉ (Edson Arantes do Nascimento)

The first thing I realised when I began compiling this list was that it is near impossible to nail down a satisfactory definition of greatness – something quantifiable or scientific. To be considered a true great requires more than just a prolific strike rate or a glistening trophy cabinet. There is no formula. Nonetheless, I boldly drew up a checklist to try to measure each player against the next.

While I naturally lean towards more attack-minded players, I have tried to ensure that these criteria took goalkeepers and centre halves into consideration too. Believe me, after the hours I've spent agonising over this list, there was no room for token inclusions – Banks and Schmeichel are as deserving of their places as Bergkamp or Beckenbauer.

Regardless of their position, I felt players needed to have displayed game-changing ability. The capacity to perform when teammates are floundering is essential if you are going to match up to the best. After all, it's great to catch the eye when the opposition are already well-beaten but the goal that breaks the deadlock, or the save that keeps it intact, is far more precious. Tight games can be a real test of a player's temperament but a certain Brazilian's focus was never in doubt.

When we came up against Brazil in the group stages of the 1970 World Cup in Mexico, we were very much the team to beat. As reigning World Champions, and with Bobby Moore in the form of his life, we looked a match for anyone. Widely, and in my view rightly, anticipated as a matchup between the two strongest teams in the tournament, the confidence and momentum that a win would bring either side would prove to be invaluable.

The game itself was incredibly tight, which came as no surprise. Today, the match is perhaps best remembered for two acts of English defiance, both coming while the score was tied at 0-0. In the first half, the result of a surging counter-attacking move, Jairzinho burst into the box and teed up Pelé for a header. He leapt and hung in the air in that inimitable way of his and directed the ball low to the right of Gordon Banks. It looked to every spectator like Brazil had found the breakthrough but, of course, you can't know the name 'Gordon Banks' without knowing that the ball did not find its way into the net. Banks thwarted Pelé, scooping the ball round the post in what has come to be viewed by many as the best save in World Cup history.

Early in the second half, with the score still goalless, Brazil began to advance towards our goal. I'd been standing among the crowd when Rivelino rocketed a free-kick past a seven-man Czech wall in their previous group game, so with Jairzinho travelling at such pace that a mistimed or misplaced limb could prove disastrous I knew it would require precision and some serious guts to dispossess him. Enter Bobby Moore. While the rest of us flinched and winced, Mooro fixed his eyes on the ball, advanced from the penalty box and slid at Jairzinho's feet. A flawless dispossession. He rose immediately to his feet and began plotting our next attack. No time to stop and enjoy the adulation.

The game rumbled on with both teams pushing for an opener and the tension ratcheting up by the minute. With the hour mark approaching, Brazil pushed forward once more. Just inside the box an off-balance Tostão looped the ball across to Pelé who was standing by the penalty spot. It fell slightly behind him but he quickly adjusted, turned to face goal and pulled back his foot, shaping to strike. The three defenders bearing down on him froze to the spot. It all took place frantically within a fraction of a second but Pelé looked serene. He trapped the ball and looked right to see Jairzinho lurking. The pass needed to be perfect; too hard and it would force him away from goal, too soft and the chance would be gone. Unfortunately, for our sake, perfection came naturally to Pelé.

Jairzinho scored and we lost by a single goal. Although both sides still progressed from the group, the Brazilians spoke openly about the confidence the win gave them. They had beaten the holders and from that point on feared no one.

Apart from the game in Mexico in '70, I was fortunate enough to play against Pelé on two more occasions for club and country – in an international friendly in '69 in the Maracanã, and in a tournament in the USA for West Ham against Santos the following September. As proud and memorable as these experiences were for me, there was a certain relief to be had in watching Pelé when you weren't directly in the firing line. During the World Cup in Mexico, as much for entertainment as for research, I watched him from the stands as Brazil took on our other group stage opponents, Czechoslovakia and Romania.

Brazil triumphed over both (as did we) with Pelé at his swaggering, unpredictable best. His confidence was evident in the experimental nature of some of his play. There is perhaps no greater testament to his success than the esteem in which some of his failures in this tournament are held. The first startling piece of unrewarded innovation came in the game against the Czechs.

More than three-and-a-half decades before a young David Beckham would attempt the same at Selhurst Park, and with a ball far less aerodynamic, Pelé picked up possession in his own half just inside the centre circle and looked up.

Spotting the keeper off his line, he launched the ball high into the air, sending it hurtling goalwards and prompting the Czech stopper to scurry back in vain. The shot narrowly missed but the moment was applauded open-mouthed by all those watching.

As daring as this effort was, the crowds in Mexico had yet to see his finest work. When Brazil took on Uruguay in the semi-finals beneath the Guadalajara sun, he deployed subtler methods to send both keeper and crowd into a state of shock. Looking to latch on to a Tostão through ball with the goalkeeper rushing out, as the two reached each other Pelé simply left the ball untouched. It was no accident and, as the goalkeeper waited and waited for the shot to come, the ball just rolled on by. Pelé, continuing and curving his run, swerved round the stranded Uruguayan to re-collect the ball but with the angle narrowing his shot skewed agonisingly wide.

It may not have resulted in a goal but it was one of the most unbelievable pieces of thought and skill I'd ever seen and was created without even touching the ball. If he had scored the goal it would have been the most wondrous thing we'd ever seen. Ron Greenwood, my old manager at West Ham, used to say, 'Simplicity is genius.' For me, Pelé was a perfect example of this. To have the foresight to even consider not touching the ball showed how devastatingly effective an uncomplicated view of the game could be. It was the one option the keeper hadn't weighed up.

The 1970 World Cup saw Pelé in his pomp as he lived up to pre-tournament predictions to claim the Golden Boot, something many great players have failed to do. In contrast, at the Swedish World Cup in 1958, Pelé's first appearance at the finals, nobody outside of Brazil expected anything from the fresh-faced seventeen-year-old.

He began the tournament nursing a knee injury on the sidelines but once he regained fitness his teammates insisted on his inclusion in the team. His World Cup debut finally arrived in the last group game, a comfortable 2-0 win over the USSR. He marked it with an assist for the second goal securing Brazil's place at the top of their group. In the next game, a quarter-final tie against Wales and with the game goalless after an hour's play, the ball came to Pelé in the area with his back to goal. Displaying all the fearlessness of a teenager, he controlled it on his chest, nicked it over a Welsh defender's toe and struck low and hard beyond the goalkeeper. Classy, calm and confident; it was a goal I'd have been proud to call my own and was enough to put Brazil through.

Next up was France in the semi-finals and Pelé was starting to get into the swing of things. Not fazed by the form of Just Fontaine (the eventual Golden Boot winner, scoring thirteen goals), the youngster continued to outperform the seasoned pros like the ringer in a pub team matchup. Fontaine already had eight goals to his name by this point compared to Pelé's solitary strike and the Brazilian was eager to make up for lost time. By full-time he had narrowed the gap by two, netting his first international hat-trick while Fontaine struck in vain, the French crashing out in a 5-2 defeat. A World Cup final against host nation Sweden awaited and Pelé was set to become the youngest ever finalist. A lot of pressure for a teenager.

By this stage, people had begun to realise that Pelé was a bit special and so his starring role in the final was less than surprising. Another 5-2 victory followed and the boy wonder added two more goals to his tally. Brazil were steamrollering their way to success but the nature of his first goal was anything but mechanical. The motion was similar to his

opening goal of the tournament versus the Welsh but the scale of the goal was simply outrageous. It was unlike any the world had ever seen; at least the world beyond Brazil.

Once again, as with many of his goals in this tournament, he received the ball on the edge of a crowded penalty area. There appeared to be no clear route to goal but he displayed the type of problem-solving that could only come from a footballing education in São Paulo. Facing a fearful huddle of defenders and with the ball slightly aloft, in one seamless move he lobbed it not over the toe (like he had against the Welsh) but over the Swede's head, before slipping past him and volleying home; audacity in the extreme.

Pelé's ability to perform so impressively and effectively at such a young age was remarkable but the way in which he continued to perform was almost superhuman. Throughout this book there are examples of players who starred at an early age, or asserted themselves as the world's greatest for short periods, but none have managed to do so for twenty years. Maradona, for all his talent, fell out of shape towards the end of his career, as did the Brazilian Ronaldo. His Portuguese namesake spent years reaching the level he's at today, and Messi has yet to replicate his club form in a World Cup. No player before or since has maintained such a high level of performance for such a sustained period.

Pelé was performing all the while for Santos too, although this was in the days before satellite television so stats, old video tapes and the firm assertions of his fellow countrymen are the main reminders of this. Every season between 1957 and 1965, Pelé was the top scorer in São Paulo's Paulista State Championship, including three seasons in which Santos failed to win the championship. While the Brazilian leagues have since been weakened by an exodus of star players to European divisions, in the 1950s and 60s Tostão

(Cruzeiro), Jairzinho, Garrincha (both Botafogo) and co. saw no need to flee their homeland and so Pelé's domestic records need no watering down. The Santos team in which Pelé starred was often described as the South American Real Madrid.

Such was the pool of talent at Brazil's disposal, to make the national side you had to be performing at the very top of your game. He'd made his debut for Santos only two years earlier, but his flashes of the sublime, the dazzling moves that left fans puzzling over what they'd just witnessed, were the key to his rapid ascent. This was something Pelé excelled in and which, to varying degrees, each of the 50 have too. Pelé played not only to win but also to entertain, an inherently Brazilian trait. This attractive approach to the game made Santos one of football's hottest properties and saw them travelling the globe to take on the best teams from other continents.

Most of these games were friendly matches but in 1962 the Intercontinental Cup pitched Benfica, the winners of the European Cup, against Santos, the Copa Libertadores winners – the South American equivalent. Brazil had just won their second consecutive World Cup in Chile but Pelé's involvement was cut short by injury. This two-legged tie gave Pelé a chance to remind Europe of his talents and show them just how good his Santos side was.

The first leg was played in Rio in the Maracanã and Santos prevailed 3-2, but Benfica were confident of overturning that score line in the return leg a month later, with more than 70,000 of their fans cheering them on. Their team was powered by the great Eusébio and they had qualified for the match by beating a Real Madrid side including Di Stéfano and Puskás in the European Cup final, so this bullishness was not without grounding.

Santos entered the game only needing a draw to win the cup, but this was not the Brazilian way. Opting for all-out attack, Pelé put in a performance of the highest quality, scoring a hat-trick and bamboozling Benfica's stars with his mazy dribbling. The game finished 5-2 and Santos were finally recognised as the greatest club side in world football. Pelé still ranks it among his greatest ever performances.

Almost in contrast to the fluid athleticism that the world came to lovingly associate with Pelé, many forget the sheer solid strength that underlaid it. As his short-lived 1966 World Cup campaign showed, players would kick Pelé and kick him hard. This wasn't special treatment, just the conditions of the time, but his robust and resilient body meant that he was still able to recover from injuries while many others would have seen their career cut short. This raises a topic that has dogged my decisions throughout this book.

Comparisons today between Messi and Ronaldo almost always factor in the difference in physical stature. It's very much a question of aesthetics but one that is essentially inconsequential. Both players have worked incredibly hard throughout their career to obtain a level of athleticism that was not gifted to them. Ronaldo's transformation into a powerful athlete is as impressive as Messi's journey to overcome severe growth deficiencies – even with hormone treatment. I'm minded to discount physical attributes from the debate altogether, as it's the way in which we utilise our strengths and adapt to overcome our weaknesses that makes the game so fascinating. The best players find a way to counterbalance their physical shortcomings with intelligence and hard work.

Any allowance for weaknesses starts to feel somewhat trivial when considering Pelé, almost like levelling the playing field to allow the mere mortals to have a go. I'm yet to be convinced that Pelé actually had any weakness. While he was no giant, standing at just 5ft 8in, he could leap higher than anyone on the pitch – and hang there too! In fact his aerial prowess was one of his greatest strengths. He was physically strong and muscular but not at the expense of mobility or agility. He had great close control but could display this at electrifying speed. He scored great goals but scored simple goals too, with over 1,000 career goals to his name. He was an unstoppable soloist but worked equally well as a team player.

For all his intelligence and talent, Pelé's most admirable attribute was that his unrelenting will to win never compromised his dignified approach to the game. The smile on his face rarely faded. Targeted with aggression and numbers by every defence he came up against, he did not dive, remonstrate or cheat. He was, and still is, a great role model and a gent.

Throughout the writing of this book I had the qualities I admire in a footballer firmly in mind; big game players, game changers, evergreens, showmen, showstoppers. Yet as I neared the top ten it became increasingly difficult to refrain from simply measuring them against Pelé, the player who had it all.

'Sure, he's good, but is he better than Pelé?'

The answer, invariably, is no.

ACKNOWLEDGEMENTS

As always, a book such as this is a product of many people's endeavours – and maybe, in this case, more so, given that this is a book of very, very subjective choices – and my choices are I know definitely not everyone else's!

My biggest thanks must go to my wife, Judith, not just for being the most wonderful of wives, but for having to continually listen to and advise on why her husband's choices of his Top 50 footballers are so obviously wrong!

Michael Sells, who so diligently listened to my choices, is the architect of the book and I thoroughly enjoyed working with this young man who I am sure has a very bright future ahead of him. And thanks to all at the Willoughby House Hotel – and especially Terry – for providing the venue for these meetings, and to all at Icon Books for pulling the whole project together.

Special thanks too to Andy Leslau who has been involved in the project from start to finish and who has, I hope, prevented me from destroying too many personal relationships while, at the same time, trying to ensure that I did not change my mind too often!

And lastly my thanks must go to all friends, players, coaches, managers, supporters and colleagues who helped me become the footballer that I became and consequently gave me the opportunity to create a book such as this. And this large group must of course also include all those players who have given me such pleasure over the years and who I have happily written about. But, maybe more importantly, I must thank all those players who you probably can't believe haven't been included in my Top 50. Thinking about it, maybe you're right and I should substitute.